Purely Formal Legal Theory

This book elaborates on deontic logic and network theory to present a reductionist theory of the law, disclosing a simple understanding of legal norms based on minimum necessary and sufficient notions. The analysis explores the concept of a 'norm' as a claim-obligation relation that regulates conduct, that is, action and inaction, among subjects, in space and time. Based on these five minimum notions, the study illustrates legal systems as networks of substantive right-duty relations that are procedurally organised according to time. The research relies on basic Kripke-style semantics as social matrixes to explain fundamental normative concepts and further on network science, social network theory and graph-theoretic notation, based on ties and nodes, to elaborate a formal representation of minimum necessary notions and of legal systems as deontic networks. The book will be of interest to academics, researchers and practitioners working in the areas of legal philosophy, legal theory and international law.

Ottavio Quirico is a senior researcher at Perugia University for Foreigners in Italy and a professor at the University of New England, Law School, in Australia and at the Australian National University, Centre for European Studies. He is also an alumnus of the European University Institute in Italy as well as a member of the Centre on Transnational Legal Relations at the Federal University of Paraiba in Brazil.

Routledge Research in Legal Philosophy

Moral Pluralism and the Complexity of Punishment
The Penal Philosophy of H.L.A. Hart
Nicolas Nayfeld

Sport, Law and Philosophy
The Jurisprudence of Sport
Miroslav Imbrisevic

Cosmopolitanism, State Sovereignty and International Law and Politics
A Theory
Jorge E. Núñez

Human Dignity, Judicial Reasoning, and the Law
Comparative Perspectives on a Key Constitutional Concept
Edited by Brett G. Scharffs, Andrea Pin, and Dmytro Vovk

Act and Omission in Criminal Law
Autonomy, Morality and Applications to Euthanasia
Roni Rosenberg

Metaethical Issues in Contemporary Legal Philosophy
A Constitutivist Approach
Edited by Stefano Bertea and Jorge Silva Sampaio

Purely Formal Legal Theory
Deontic Networks
Ottavio Quirico

For more information about this series, please visit: https://www.routledge.com/Routledge-Research-in-Legal-Philosophy/book-series/RRLP

Purely Formal Legal Theory

Deontic Networks

Ottavio Quirico

Routledge
Taylor & Francis Group
LONDON AND NEW YORK

First published 2025
by Routledge
4 Park Square, Milton Park, Abingdon, Oxon OX14 4RN

and by Routledge
605 Third Avenue, New York, NY 10158

Routledge is an imprint of the Taylor & Francis Group, an informa business

British Library Cataloguing-in-Publication Data
A catalogue record for this book is available from the British Library

Library of Congress Cataloging-in-Publication Data
Names: Quirico, Ottavio, author.
Title: Purely formal legal theory : deontic networks / Ottavio Quirico.
Description: Abingdon, Oxon [UK] ; New York, NY : Routledge, 2025. | Series: Routledge research in legal philosophy | Includes bibliographical references and index.
Identifiers: LCCN 2024054246 (print) | LCCN 2024054247 (ebook) | ISBN 9781032132488 (hardback) | ISBN 9781032132518 (paperback) | ISBN 9781003228318 (ebook)
Subjects: LCSH: Law—Philosophy. | State, The. | International law. | Law—European Union countries. | Deontic logic.
Classification: LCC K231 .Q85 2025 (print) | LCC K231 (ebook) | DDC 340/.1511314—dc23/eng/20241118
LC record available at https://lccn.loc.gov/2024054246
LC ebook record available at https://lccn.loc.gov/2024054247

ISBN: 978-1-032-13248-8 (hbk)
ISBN: 978-1-032-13251-8 (pbk)
ISBN: 978-1-003-22831-8 (ebk)

DOI: 10.4324/9781003228318

Typeset in Times New Roman
by Apex CoVantage, LLC

To G.

Contents

Abbreviations

BCE	before common era
CFSP	Common Foreign and Security Policy
CJEU	Court of Justice of the European Union
COPUOS	Committee on the Peaceful Uses of Outer Space
CRDS	Convention on the Rights and Duties of States
CREFAA	Convention on the Recognition and Enforcement of Foreign Arbitral Awards
DARIO	Draft Articles on the Responsibility of International Organizations
DASR	Draft Articles on State Responsibility
DSU	Dispute Settlement Understanding
EC	European Commission
ECJ	European Court of Justice
ECSC	European Coal and Steel Community
EEC	European Economic Community
EEZ	exclusive economic zone
EU	European Union
Euratom	European Atomic Energy Community
GATT	General Agreement on Trade and Tariffs
IBRD	International Bank for Reconstruction and Development
ICC	International Criminal Court
ICJ	International Court of Justice
ILC	International Law Commission
MFN	most-favoured-nation
NGO	non-governmental organisation
OJ	official journal
PCIJ	Permanent Court of International Justice
PJCC	Police and Judicial Cooperation in Criminal Matters
TEEC	Treaty Establishing the European Economic Community
TEU	Treaty on European Union
TFEU	Treaty on the Functioning of the European Union
UEA	Uniform Evidence Act

UK	United Kindgom
UN	United Nations
UNCLOS	United Nations Convention on the Law of the Sea
UP	University Press
US	United States
USSR	Union of Soviet Socialist Republics
UTC	universal time coordinated
VCCISG	Vienna Convention on Contracts for the International Sale of Goods
VCLT	Vienna Convention on the Law of Treaties
VCLTIO	Vienna Convention on the Law of Treaties between States and International Organizations or between International Organizations
WTO	World Trade Organization

Introduction

A purely formal legal theory

The meaning of 'science' is debated, to the extent that the existence of a conclusive definition can be denied in favour of an anarchist approach to scientific methodology.[1] Against this valuable sceptical background, 'science' can be narrowly regarded as knowledge about the structure and behaviour of the natural and physical world, based on facts that can be proved, that is, verified or falsified, especially by way of experiments.[2] Although this definition can apply to social sciences, so much so that its extension to at least certain elements of economics has been supported,[3] it does not easily apply to the law. More broadly, 'science' can be conceived of as a system for organising knowledge about a particular subject, thus elaborating explanatory, taxonomic, unifying and predictive theories.[4] This definition easily applies to

1 P. Feyerabend, *Against Method*, New Left Books, 1975, Verso, 2002, at 11; P. Feyerabend, *The Tyranny of Science*, Polity Press, 2011, at 6.

2 See K. Popper, *Conjectures and Refutations: The Growth of Scientific Knowledge*, 1993, Routledge, Reprint 2004, at 43 ff.; H. Sankey, 'Scientific Method', in M. Curd and S. Psillos (eds.), *The Routledge Companion to Philosophy of Science*, Routledge, 2014, 280.

3 U. Mäki, 'Economics', in M. Curd and S. Psillos (eds.), *The Routledge Companion*, Routledge, 2014, 621, at 633.

4 See P. Feyerabend, *Realism, Rationalism and Scientific Method*, Cambridge University Press, 1981, at 55; P. Feyerabend, *Problems of Empiricism*, Cambridge University Press, 1981, at 57; K.D. Bailey, *Typologies and Taxonomies: An Introduction to Classification Techniques*, Sage, 1994; L. von Bertalanffy, *General System Theory: Foundations, Development, Applications*, G. Braziller, 2003; H. Kincaid, 'Social Sciences', in Curd and Psillos (eds.), *The Routledge Companion*, 2014, 672; C. Kwa, *Styles of Knowing: A New History of Science from Ancient Times to the Present*, Pittsburgh Press, 2021.

DOI: 10.4324/9781003228318-1

human behaviour and society (practical reason)[5] and, thus, certainly applies to the law.[6]

Within this framework, a first question concerns the ascertainment of the extent of legal knowledge: different answers are possible. Schematically, three approaches can be adopted: an ontological perspective, a deontological approach and a sociological view.[7] The first approach studies the law as it is ('ontic deontic').[8] The second perspective considers the law as it should be, in its relationship with ethics ('meta-deontic').[9] The third approach considers the law in its relationship with social inputs ('social deontic' or 'legal phenomenology').[10] The deontological and sociological approaches are more extensive and do not study the law in a vacuum. By contrast, the ontological approach studies the law as it is, as a 'pure science', and is therefore more limited, whereby 'law as it is' refers to the 'law as it is created by existing authorities', and the ontological approach is thus a positivistic science,[11] which is ultimately grounded in the foundational concept of a basic rule (*Grundnorm*).[12] In light of this, the law is certainly problematic, especially because the limits of positivistic law cannot be clearly defined.

5 I. Kant, 'Die Metaphysik der Sitten (Groundwork of the Metaphysics of Morals)', 1979, in M. Gregor (tr.), *Practical Philosophy: Works of Immanuel Kant*, Cambridge University Press, 1997, 37, at 101; M. Weber, 'Die "Objektivität" sozialwissenschaftlicher und sozialpolitischer Erkenntnis (The Objectivity of Knowledge in Social Science and Social Policy)', 1904, in H.H. Bruun and S. Whimster (eds.), *Max Weber: Collected Methodological Writings*, Routledge, 2012, 100, at 107; J. Habermas, *Zur Logik der Sozialwissenschaften (On the Logic of Social Sciences)*, Suhrkamp Verlag, 1982, tr. S.W. Nicholsen and J.A. Stark, Polity Press, 1988; P. Ricoeur, 'Herméneutique et sciences sociales', in P. Amselek (ed.), *Théorie du droit et science*, PUF, 1994, 15, at 18; R. Carnap, *The Unity of Science*, Thoemmes Press, 1995, at 42; K. Brad Wray, 'Social Epistemology', in Curd and Psillos (eds.), *The Routledge Companion*, 2014, 112.

6 Popper, *Conjectures*, 1993, at 341 ff. See also C. Calhoun and D. Rhote, 'Integrating the Social Sciences: Theoretical Knowledge, Methodological Tools, and Practical Applications', in R. Frodeman, J.T. Klein and C. Mitcham (eds.), *The Oxford Handbook of Interdisciplinarity*, Oxford University Press, 2010, 103; P.L. Gentili, *Untangling Complex Systems*, CRC Press, 2019, at 16.

7 See N. Bobbio, *Teoria generale del diritto* (*General Theory of Law*), Giappichelli, 1993, at 23 ff.

8 Bobbio, *Teoria generale*, 1993, at 23 ff. See further H. Kelsen, *Reine Rechtslehre* (*Pure Theory of Law*), UC Press, 1934, tr. M. Knight, 1989, at 1.

9 Bobbio, *Teoria generale*, 1993, at 23 ff. See further D. Hume, *A Treatise of Human Nature*, 1739, Clarendon Press, 1896, at 483; S. von Pufendorf, *De Officio Hominis et Civis Juxta Legem Naturalem Libri Duo* (*On the Duty of Man and Citizen according to Natural Law*), 1673, tr. M. Silverthorne, Cambridge University Press, 1991, at 33.

10 Bobbio, *Teoria generale*, 1993, at 23 ff. See further E. Erlich, *Grundlegung der Soziologie des Rechts*, Dunker, 1913; T. Carbonnier, *Sociologie juridique*, 1979, PUF, 1994, at 13 ff.; N. Luhmann, *Das Recht der Gesellschaft (Law as a Social System)*, Suhrkamp, 1993, tr. K.A. Ziegert, Oxford University Press, 2004, at 464.

11 J. Austin, *The Province of Jurisprudence Determined*, Murray, 1832, Weidenfeld & Nicolson, 1954, at 9; G. Sartor, P. Casanovas, M.A. Biasiotti and M. Fernández-Barrera (eds.), *Approaches to Legal Ontologies: Theories, Domains, Methodologies*, Springer, 2011.

12 Kelsen, *Reine Rechtslehre (Pure Theory)*, 1934, at 201.

However, the establishment of the limits of legal science is even more problematic from a deontological and sociological perspective, which is definitely broader. The analysis developed in this book is confined to an ontological perspective. A second question concerns the choice of the tools through which it is possible to organise (ontological) legal knowledge. Once again, different answers are viable, depending on the chosen principles. The fundamental idea of the present research is achieving maximum simplicity in understanding the law and its ramifications.[13] Therefore, the choice is to rely on minimum and elementary concepts[14] in order to elaborate a structured theory (modelling)[15] for positive law.

In sum, this monograph develops a concise inquiry into ontological (positivistic) legal theory and further applies theoretical notions to the areas of international law and European Union (EU) law.[16] The 'general theory of law' or 'legal theory' can be understood as the analysis of the law, as a whole, through its fundamental concepts.[17] From this standpoint, essential notions, particularly the concept of a 'norm' or 'rule', belong to general legal theory because they provide a basis for organising the normative legal order and facilitate its comprehension as a system: the law is a normative and practical science.[18] As a result, the concept of a 'rule' is also essential to understanding international law and EU law as specific normative ramifications, in the light of the concept of 'sovereignty'.[19] Several studies have been developed in legal theory on normative systems and regulation from different perspectives. For instance, while Austin, Kelsen and Hart considered legal rules and normative systems from a positivistic angle,[20] exploring matters such as their foundation and validity, Sen and Rawls delved more into (moral, social, economic and political) questions of interest and justice supporting the rule of law, including

13 'If you can't explain it simply, you don't understand it well enough' (A. Einstein). See further W. Van Orman Quine, 'On Simple Theories of a Complex World', in J.R. Gregg and F.T.C. Harris (eds.), *Form and Strategy in Science*, D. Reided Publishing Company, 1964, 47.

14 'Entia non sunt multiplicanda praeter necessitatem' (W. of Ockham, *Summa Totius Logicae*, 1323, I, at 12).

15 'Ces longues chaînes de raisons, toutes simples et faciles, dont les géomètres ont coutume de se servir pour parvenir à leurs plus difficiles démonstrations, m'avaient donné occasion de m'imaginer que toutes les choses, qui peuvent tomber sous la connaissance des hommes, s'entre-suivent en même façon' (R. Descartes, *Discours de la Méthode*, A Leyde de l'Imprimerie de Ian Maire, 1637, at II). See also H. Heyck, *Age of Systems*, John Hopkins University Press, 2015, at 165 ff.

16 'As to the shortness of the book, I am awfully sorry for it: if you were to squeeze me like a lemon, you would get nothing more out of me' (L. Wittgenstein, *Tractatus Logico-Philosophicus*, Cambridge University Press, 1922, Supplements).

17 See J.-L. Bergel, *Théorie générale du droit*, LGDJ, 2003, at 3–4.

18 C.S. Peirce, 'An Outline Classification of the Sciences, 1903', in N. Houser and C.J.W. Kloesel (eds.), *The Essential Peirce*, Indiana University Press, 1998, Vol. II, 258, at 259.

19 H. Kelsen, *General Theory of Law and State*, Russell & Russell, 1945, at 328 ff.; H. Hart, *The Concept of Law*, 1961, Clarendon Press, 3rd ed., 2012, at 220 ff.

20 Fundamentally, Kelsen outlined a 'geometrically structured' conception of the law akin to the model developed by Kant in the field of ethics (see Kant, 'Die Metaphysik der Sitten', 1997, at 43).

economic considerations and the principles underpinning the social contract accepted by free, equal and rational persons.[21]

Against such a background, this book aims to make an innovative contribution to legal theory by developing a formal analysis of (ontological) legal concepts. More precisely, the book seeks to investigate legal semiotics and unveil hidden logical legal structures—that is, 'legally signified' meanings.[22] In the light of Peirce's triadic theory of the sign, the analysis is based on the assumption that the law is ultimately not a matter of words (natural language), but rather a matter of conceptual forms (iconic signs).[23] More specifically, two methods are taken into account: deontic logic and network analysis, which are combined in order to formalise deontic concepts via network theory. The idea is thus elaborating a model (paradigm) for the law based on formalised essential deontic tools, whereby, as a result, legal knowledge should be understood as a synthetic formal network and, more specifically, as a *formal deontic network*, within the framework of a formal network theory of the law, which is computational (mechanical) and can be synthesised via Kripke-style semantics (Claim_{p1}(non)A—Obl_{p2}(non)A) and graph-theoretic notation (• — •).[24]

Overall, this work simply discloses *a purely formal theory of the law*, to the extent that it unveils the possibility of conceiving of the law and legal systems based exclusively on formal concepts and, thus, as a formal stream of thoughts.[25] It further shows the potential of such a vision by exploring some fundamental implications with respect to the specific areas of international law and EU law, based on the notions of 'State' and 'sovereignty' as fundamental units of legal thinking. This vision should contribute to elaborating a consistent systematisation of legal logic, 'mapping' the law as a formal system.[26]

21 J. Rawls, *A Theory of Justice*, Belknap Press at Harvard University Press, revised ed., 1999, at 10; A. Sen, *The Idea of Justice*, Belknap Press of Harvard University Press, 2009. See further R. Lucas, 'On the Mechanics of Economic Development' (1988) 22(1) *Journal of Monetary Economics* 3.

22 See H.A. Lloyd, 'How to Do Things with Signs: Semiotics in Legal Theory, Practice, and Education' (2021) 55 *University of Richmond Law Review* 861, at 862.

23 'Firstly, there are likenesses, or icons; which serve to convey ideas of the things they represent simply by imitating them' (C.S. Peirce, 'What Is a Sign?', 1894, in N. Houser and C.J.W. Kloesel (eds.), *The Essential Peirce*, 1998, Vol. II, 4, at 5–10).

24 See S. Kripke, 'Semantical Considerations on Modal Logic' (1963) 16 *Acta Philosophica Fennica* 83; J.F. Sowa, *Knowledge Representation: Logical, Philosophical and Computational Representation*, Brooks/Cole, 2000; J.-P. Dupuy, *On the Origin of Cognitive Science: The Mechanisation of the Mind*, tr. M.B. DeBevoise, MIT Press, 2009, at 3; S. Sonawane, P.N. Mahalle and A.S. Ghotka (eds.), *Information Retrieval and Natural Language Processing: A Graph Theory Approach*, Springer, 2022, at 1 ff.

25 'All seeing is essentially perspective, and so is all knowing' (F. Nietzsche, *Genealogy of Morals*, Broadview Press, 1887).

26 'Study the art of science, study the science of art. Develop your senses, especially learn how to see. Realise that everything connects to everything else' (Leonardo da Vinci).

The analysis is therefore divided into two parts. First, the book explores and illustrates a simplified and formalised conception of fundamental legal tools, visualising a 'deontic network' (P—P). Second, in the light of the basic notion of 'sovereignty', the analysis applies such concepts to specific mechanisms under international law and EU law.

1 Norm

1.1 Schematic deontic logic

Deontic logic, which is concerned with normative duties,[1] considers the law as a set of modalities governing human conduct: that is, praxis (from Greek *πρᾶξις*: action).[2] The adjective 'deontic' comes from the Greek verb '*δεί*', which means 'being obligatory' or 'being due'. In fact, deontic logic can be defined as the field of logic that is concerned with obligations, permissions and related concepts. Early deontic logic dates to the time of Ancient Greece and the late Middle Ages. However, the first specific investigations into the discipline were developed by Mally in 1926 and the final outbreak of this branch of philosophical logic can be traced back to the second half of the 20th century, particularly to the work of Von Wright, Becker and Kalinowski.[3]

Deontic logic posits that there are the 'deontic modes' or 'modes of obligation', including notions such as the 'obligatory (that which we ought to do)', the 'permitted (that which we are allowed to do)', and the 'forbidden (that which we must not do)'.[4] The very basic building blocks of deontic logic are therefore the notions of 'obligation', 'prohibition' and 'permission'; 'being obligatory', 'being forbidden' and 'being permitted' are the three fundamental deontic statuses for acting or omitting $\left(P_{\rightarrow(\text{no})\text{act}}\right)$, that is, for performing or not performing specific conduct.[5] Deontic logic therefore studies propositions about what is obligatory, permitted, forbidden and derivative deontic features of conduct.[6]

1 J. Kalinowski, *Études de logique déontique I, 1953–1969*, Gallica, 1972, at 185.

2 See Kalinowski, *Études de logique déontique I*, 1972, at 19; G. Sartor, *Legal Reasoning: A Cognitive Approach to the Law*, Springer, 2007, at 453 ff.

3 See P.E. Navarro and J.L. Rodrigues, *Deontic Logic and Legal Systems*, Cambridge University Press, 2014, at 3 ff.; C. Peterson, *De la logique des obligations, des permissions et des interdictions: de Von Wright à aujourd'hui*, Presses de l'Université de Montréal, 2016, at 7 ff.

4 G.H. Von Wright, 'Deontic Logic' (1951) 60 *Mind* 1.

5 Von Wright, 'Deontic Logic', 1951, at 2.

6 Von Wright, 'Deontic Logic', 1951, at 2; Kalinowski, *Études de logique déontique I*, 1972, at 21.

DOI: 10.4324/9781003228318-2

Stating that conduct is 'obligatory' means that it is 'due', is 'mandatory', is 'compulsory', 'must be held' or 'must be performed'.[7] This modality overlaps with that of a 'duty'[8] and can be expressed through symbolic propositional logic,[9] notably via Kripke-style semantics.[10]

$\boldsymbol{Obl}_p$A (it is obligatory for a person (*p*) to act, e.g., to pay)
$\boldsymbol{Obl}_p$NON-A (it is obligatory for *p* not to act, e.g., not to smoke)

whereby **Obl** is the 'deontic' modality of an 'obligation' and A stands for 'action'.

The concept of a 'prohibition' is complementary to that of an 'obligation'. 'Being forbidden' or 'being prohibited' is the modality of action that should not be performed.[11]

This can be expressed via symbolic notation.

$\boldsymbol{Forb}_p$A (A is forbidden for *p*, e.g., it is forbidden for *p* to smoke)

Fundamentally, however, the concept of a 'prohibition' is absorbed into that of an 'obligation'. In fact, the modality of a 'prohibition' is nothing other than the negative formulation of an 'obligation'.

$\boldsymbol{Forb}_p$A = $\boldsymbol{Obl}_p$NON-A (it is forbidden for *p* to smoke = it is obligatory for *p* not to smoke)
$\boldsymbol{Forb}_p$NON-A = $\boldsymbol{Obl}_p$A (it is forbidden for *p* not to pay = it is obligatory for *p* to pay)

whereby **Forb** is the deontic modality of a 'prohibition', **Obl** is the deontic modality of an 'obligation' and A stands for 'action'.

7 Kalinowski, *Études de logique déontique I*, 1972, at 91.

8 A. Ross, *Om ret og retfærdighed (On Law and Justice)*, 1953, University of California Press, 1958, at 162.

9 See A.N. Whithead and B. Russell, *Principia Mathematica*, Cambridge University Press, 1910–1913; E. Husserl, *Formale und transzendentale Logik. Versuch einer Kritik der logischen Vernunft (Formal and Transcendental Logic)*, 1929, tr. T.D. Carins, Springer, 1969, at 48; M. Sainsbury, *Logical Forms: An Introduction to Philosophical Logic*, Blackwell, 2nd ed., 2001, at 339; W.G. Frege, 'Conceptual Notation (1879)', in A. Sullivan (ed.), *Logicism and the Philosophy of Language*, Broadview Press, 2003, 93; D. Westerståhl, *Foundations of Logic: Completeness, Incompleteness, Computability*, CSLI Publications, 2023, at 11.

10 Kripke, 'Semantical Considerations' (1963) at 83; S. Kripke, *Philosophical Troubles*, Oxford University Press, 2011, at 75; A. Rotolo and G. Sartor, 'Deductive and Deontic Reasoning', in G. Bongiovanni, G. Postema, A. Rotolo, G. Sartor, C. Valentini and D. Walton (eds.), *Handbook of Legal Reasoning and Argumentation*, Springer, 2018, 243, at 252–253.

11 Ross, *Om ret*, 1958, at 162.

The concept of a 'permission' means 'the possibility of an action and its omission'.[12] The modality of a 'permission' can be expressed through various propositions: 'it is permitted'; 'it is legal'; 'it is allowed'; 'it is possible'; 'a subject is empowered'. Therefore, the idea of a 'permission' overlaps with those of a 'faculty', 'right' and 'power'. The modality of a 'permission' can be expressed through Kripke-style semantics.

> $\boldsymbol{Perm}_p$A/NON-A (A or NON-A is permitted for *p*, e.g., it is permitted for *p* to smoke or not to smoke)

whereby **Perm** is the deontic modality of a 'permission', and A is positive (or negative) conduct.

Finally, if it is assumed that an 'obligation' is the positive modality of a 'prohibition', the former status encompasses the latter, and we are thus left with two fundamental deontic modalities: 'permission' $\left(P_{perm \rightarrow (no)act}\right)$ and 'obligation' $\left(P_{obl \rightarrow (no)act}\right)$.

This is a very basic approach to deontic logic. In fact, more sophisticated distinctions can be established and various logical connections can be outlined between heterogeneous deontic modalities. In particular, the relationship between the conditions of 'permission', 'right', 'faculty' and 'power' on the one hand and those of an 'obligation' and a 'duty' on the other hand can be further explored.[13] Along these lines, a sophisticated distinction has clearly been elaborated to explain jural relationships, involving the concepts of 'right', 'privilege', 'power' and 'immunity' on the one hand and those of 'no-right', 'duty', 'disability' and 'liability' on the other.[14] Thus, the notion of P_1's contracted privilege of accessing owned property would match P_2's 'no-right' that P_1 does not access owned property.[15]

The present analysis aims to keep argumentation as simple as possible,[16] building on the idea that conduct that is 'permitted' for a person (P_1) is a 'claim' and is necessarily matched by the correlated 'obligation' of another person (P_2). Indeed, even detailed analyses of logical concepts ultimately acknowledge that a legal duty or obligation outlines what one ought to do rather than not, whereby 'duty' and 'right' are necessarily correlated notions,

12 Sartor, *Legal Reasoning*, 2007, at 459.

13 See, for instance, B.S. Jackson, *Semiotics and Legal Theory*, Routledge and Keagan Paul, 1985, at 100 ff.

14 W.N. Hohfeld, 'Some Fundamental Legal Conceptions as Applied in Judicial Reasoning' (1913) *Yale Law Journal* 16, at 30; Ross, *Om ret*, 1958, at 161–162.

15 Hohfeld, 'Some Fundamental Legal Conceptions' (1913) at 33.

16 Van Orman Quine, 'On Simple Theories', 1964, at 48.

so much so that when a right is breached, a duty is infringed.[17] Thus, the idea is bringing the notion of an 'obligation' to the fore as the core of a legal norm in its connection to the behaviour of a person, whereby the notion of a claim—obligation (or obligation—claim) relationship is streamlined as the essential function of the law, that is, binding persons through a normative bond.[18]

A simplified approach to deontic concepts, based on the correlated notions of 'claim' and 'obligation', can be expressed through Kripke-style semantics.

> $\boldsymbol{Perm}_{p1}$(NON)A – $\boldsymbol{Obl}_{p2}$(NON)A (it is permitted for p_1 (not) to smoke) – (it obligatory for p_2 to let p_1 (elect not to) smoke)

1.2 Norm: claim, obligation, right and duty

Given that it sets an obligation, in general legal theory, a 'norm' (from the Greek '*νόμος*': 'rule') is fundamentally qualified as a prescriptive proposition, which is the ultimate basis of deontic logic.[19] However, a norm or rule can exist with or without words. For instance, the rules of the road are mostly formulated through non-verbal signs and gestures can express imperative commands.[20] Nonetheless, as natural language, which is a verbal system of signs working through dialogic conversation, is the 'medium through which law acts',[21] a norm can always be enunciated through words and utterances,[22] and thus a normative proposition can be considered the basic foundation for a lawyer's thinking.[23] In any case, as it is prescriptive, a norm necessarily entails the idea of a claim matching an obligation, regardless of the way in which it is expressed, governing conduct (action or inaction) among persons:[24] it obligatory to behave 'rightly', that is, according to the norms (normally: rule of conduct).[25]

17 Hohfeld, 'Some Fundamental Legal Conceptions' (1913) at 32; Ross, *Om ret*, 1958, at 163.

18 See H. Kelsen, *Reine Rechtslehre (Introduction to the Problems of Legal Theory)*, F. Duticke, 1934, tr. Paulson, Clarendon Press, 1992, at 42–43.

19 See N. Bobbio, *Essais de théorie du droit*, eds. M. Guéret, C. Agostini and R. Guastini, Bruylant, 1998, at 117–118.

20 See R. Kevelson, *The Law as a System of Signs*, Plenum Publishing, 1988, at 4; A. Sériaux, *Le droit – Une introduction*, Ellipses, 1997, at 254.

21 B. Brix, *Law, Language and Legal Determinacy*, Clarendon Press, 1993, at 1; H.E.S. Mattila, 'Legal Vocabulary', in P.M. Tiersma and L.M. Solan (eds.), *The Oxford Handbook of Language and Law*, Oxford University Press, 2012, at 27.

22 See F.K. Savigny, *Vom Beruf unserer Zeit für Gesetzgebung und Rechtswissenschaft*, Ben Mohr und Bimmer, 1814; Ross, *Om ret*, 1958, at 6–7 and 111 ff.; Kevelson, *The Law as a System*, 1988, at 5; S.A. Hetcher, *Norms in a Wired World*, Cambridge University Press, 2004, at 18; A. Marmor, *The Language of Law*, Oxford University Press, 2014, at 11.

23 See Bobbio, *Essais*, 1998, at 2–3 and 7–8.

24 See M. Virally, *La pensée juridique*, LGDJ, 1960, at 47–49.

25 J. Raz, *Practical Reason and Norms*, Princeton University Press, 1970, Oxford University Press, 2002, at 49; J.-F. Perrin, *Pour une théorie de la connaissance juridique*, Droz, 1979,

Following a minimalistic (reductionist) approach,[26] it is possible to rely on a simplified view of deontic tools and analytically to divide the concept of a 'norm' into three basic elements: claim—obligation relationship (1: Claim—Obl), persons (2: P) and conduct (3: $P_{\rightarrow(\text{no})\text{act}}$). Thus, a norm can be seen as a claim—obligation (or obligation—claim) relationship that regulates conduct (action or inaction) among persons.

> **Norm**: $\boldsymbol{Claim}_{p1}$(NON)A – $\boldsymbol{Obl}_{p2}$(NON)A (p_1 has a claim (to elect not) to smoke) – (p_2 is obliged to let p_1 (elect not to) smoke)

Building on this schematism $\left(P_{1\text{claim}\rightarrow(\text{no})\,\text{act}—\text{act}(\text{no})\leftarrow\text{obl}_2}P\right)$,[27] it is conceivable that a norm regulates a claim—obligation relationship between two or more persons.[28] Thus, a balanced distinction between active and passive legal modalities can be grounded in four minimum and correlated positions: 'claim' and 'right' on the one hand and 'obligation' and 'duty' on the other. Within such a framework, the concepts of a 'claim' and a 'right' define active positions, whereas those of an 'obligation' and a 'duty' outline passive situations.

The literature dwells on the notion of a 'subjective right',[29] which is conceived of as a prerogative of a right-holder protected by the law[30]—that is, the side of a legal relationship that is favourable to a person[31]—and refers to the concepts of a 'right', 'duty', 'claim' and 'obligation' alternatively. In this context, dealing with the relational aspect of the law, the correspondence between the notions of a 'right' and a 'claim' on the one hand and those of a 'duty' and an 'obligation' on the other is highlighted.[32] Notably, it is often considered that the concept of a 'right' is necessarily correlated to that of an 'obligation' and that 'rights' and 'obligations' exhaust objective law, whereby 'the legal right of one subject' would be 'merely the reflex of the legal obligation of another subject', underscoring the primary importance of the concept of a

---

at 27; H. Kelsen, *Allgemeine Theorie der Normen (General Theory of Norms)*, Manz Verlag, 1979, Oxford University Press, 1991, at 3; K.N. Llewellyn, *The Theory of Rules*, University of Chicago Press, 2011, at 87.

26 'Frustra fit per multa quod potest fieri per pauciora' (W. of Ockham, *Summa*, 1323, I, at 12). See also M. Fried, 'Art and Objecthood' (1967) 6(2) *Artforum* 12.

27 See D. Walton, C. Reed and F. Macagno, *Argumentation Schemes*, Cambridge University Press, 2008, at 321.

28 See Virally, *La pensée juridique*, 1960, at 49–50.

29 G.W.F. Hegel, *Philosophie des Rechts (Philosophy of Rights)*, 1820, tr. S.W. Dyde, Batoche Books, 2001, at 51; H. Dedek, 'Subjective Right(s)', in J.M. Smits, J. Husa, C. Valcke and M. Narciso (eds.), *Encyclopaedia of Comparative Law*, Edward Elgar, 2024, 449.

30 See, for instance, Kelsen, *Reine Rechtslehre* (*Pure Theory)*, 1934, at 125–127.

31 Ross, *Om ret*, 1958, at 175.

32 See, for instance, Virally, *La pensée juridique*, 1960, at 43–44.

'right'.[33] However, for the purpose of clarity, we can consider that the notions of a 'claim' and an 'obligation' outline correlated bilateral positions, whereas those of a 'right' and a 'duty' define multilateral positions. Indeed, the terms 'claim' and 'obligation' are more commonly employed on a bilateral scale, whereas those of a 'right' and a 'duty' are more commonly used as correlated notions on a general scale,[34] whereby a consistent distinction between these concepts can lead to a clearer understanding of legal positions.[35]

Moreover, the concepts of a 'right' and a 'duty' outline particular structures when they bind a person vis-à-vis some other (determined) persons in a specific legal order, whereas they outline universal—or general—structures when they link a person vis-à-vis all other (undetermined) persons in a specific legal order. Therefore, rights and duties bind a subject towards some or all of the other subjects in a specific legal order.[36] A 'right' can thus be conceived of as an aggregation of 'claims', permitting specific conduct $\left(\text{A or NON-A: } P_{\rightarrow(\text{no})\text{act}}\right)$, which a person holds vis-à-vis some or all of the other persons in a specific legal order $\left(P_{1\ \text{right}\rightarrow(\text{no})\text{act}\leftarrow\text{obl}}P_{2,3\ldots}\right)$. In turn, a 'duty' can be regarded as an aggregation of 'obligations', compelling specific conduct $\left(\text{A or NON-A: } P_{\rightarrow(\text{no})\text{act}}\right)$, which a person owes vis-à-vis some or all of the other persons in a specific legal order $\left(P_{1\ \text{duty}\rightarrow(\text{no})\ \text{act}\leftarrow\ \text{claim}}\ P_{2,3\ldots}\right)$. Four situations thus emerge: relative right, absolute right, relative duty and absolute duty. A right is relative when it links a person to a determinate number of persons, whereas it is absolute when it links a person to all the (undetermined) persons of a particular legal order. Symmetrically, a duty is relative when it links a person to a determinate number of persons, whereas it is absolute when it links a person to all the (undetermined) persons of a given legal order.[37]

The normative concepts of a 'right' and a 'duty' can be expressed through Kripke-style semantics.

> ***Right***$_{p1}$(NON)A – ***Obl***$_{p2,p3\ldots}$(NON)A (p_1 has the right (not) to smoke) – (p_2, p_3 . . . are obliged to let p_1 (elect not to) smoke)
> ***Claim***$_{p1,p2\ldots}$(NON)A – ***Duty***$_{p3}$(NON)A (p_1, p_2 . . . are permitted (not) to smoke) – (p_3 has a duty to let p_1 and p_2 (elect not to) smoke)

Analytically, it is possible to outline this pattern: an absolute right—duty relationship binds a person towards all the other persons of a specific legal

33 Kelsen, *Reine Rechtslehre (Introduction)*, 1934, at 42 and 44.
34 See, for instance, Kelsen, *General Theory*, 1945, at 58, 75 and 77.
35 C.S. Peirce, 'How to Make Our Ideas Clear, 1878', in N. Houser and C.J.W. Kloesel (eds.), *The Essential Peirce*, 1992, vol. I, 124.
36 Austin, *The Province of Jurisprudence*, 1832, at 18–22; Kelsen, *General Theory*, 1945, at 86.
37 See Kelsen, *General Theory*, 1945, at 75 ff., especially at 136–137.

order and encompasses a set of claim—obligation relationships.[38] In other words, an absolute right embeds the totality of the claims governing specific conduct that a person holds vis-a-vis all the other persons within a given legal order, whereas an absolute duty encompasses the totality of the obligations governing specific conduct that a person holds vis-à-vis all the other persons within a given legal order.

In the light of this pattern, the foundation, that is, the basic unit—or principle—of every legal structure, is the claim—obligation (or obligation—claim) or right—duty (or duty—right) relationship, which are concepts that can be understood in a relative or absolute sense.[39] Therefore, a norm can be conceived of as a right—duty (or claim—obligation) relationship (1) that regulates conduct (action or inaction) (2) among persons (3) $\left(P_{1,2\ldots\ \text{claim(right)}\rightarrow\text{(no) act}\text{—}\text{act(no)}\leftarrow\text{(duty)obl}\ldots 4,3}P\right)$.

1.3 Legal personality

Given that norms govern claims, obligations, rights and duties between persons, who are the addressees of such rules, 'legal personality'—also known as 'legal capacity'—can be defined as the ability to have rights and duties[40] and is thus the ability to have legal relationships—that is, claim—obligation (or obligation—claim) and right—duty (or duty—right) relationships—vis-à-vis other persons. Therefore, 'persons' are distinguished from things (*res*), which are physical items governed by claims, obligations, rights and duties.[41] Indeed, the concept of 'legal personality' identifies a person who can be a 'subject of the law': that is, a unit that can be attributed claims, obligations, rights and duties.[42] Within this framework, while a human being is easily seen as a separate right-holder (P), organisational entities also can.[43] Therefore, a person (P_1) has, for instance, a right to property, which is matched by the obligations of other persons (P_2, P_3, P_4 . . .), not to interfere with such a right. Additionally, persons can have 'legal competence' (P_{comp})—or 'power' (P_{pow})[44]—that is, the ability to act in order to create, vary or remove claims, obligations, rights and

38 See R. Drago, 'La notion d'obligation: droit public et droit privé' (2000) 44 *Archives de philosophie du droit* 43.

39 Drago, 'La notion d'obligation' (2000) at 44.

40 T. Pietrzykowsky, 'Law, Persons and the Discontents of Juridical Humanism', in T. Pietrzykowsky and B. Stancioli (eds.), *New Approaches to the Personhood in Law: Essays in Legal Philosophy*, Peter Lang GmbH, Internationaler Verlag der Wissenschaften, 2016, 13.

41 V.A.J. Kurki, *A Theory of Legal Personhood*, Oxford University Press, 2019, at 12.

42 Kelsen, *Reine Rechtslehre* (*Pure Theory*), 1934, at 168–170.

43 T. Pietrzykowsky and B. Stancioli, 'Modern Challenges to the Concept of a Person in Law', in Pietrzykowsky and Stancioli (eds.), *New Approaches*, 2016, 7.

44 Ross, *Om ret*, 1958, at 166.

duties.[45] Some scholars speak, in this regard, of 'passive' and 'active' legal personhood, respectively, identifying the capacity to have rights and duties and the capacity to act and create, vary or remove rights and duties.[46]

'Legal subjectivity' or 'legal capacity'—that is, 'legal personhood' (P)—underpins 'the conceptual space for modern law' and generates the concept of a 'subjective right'.[47] Thus, it is considered that legal personhood entails the capacity to have at least a single legal right.[48] Within this framework, individuals, and thus human beings, are physical—or natural—persons who have legal capacity, provided they have been born and are alive and sentient.[49] These can aggregate and constitute legal entities—notably, corporations, non-governmental organisations (NGOs), States and international organisations—which are 'juristic' or 'legal' persons.[50] As they have no physical sphere of existence, non-physical legal persons are merely juristic constructs and are thus defined as 'artificial' persons.[51] Sometimes, the expression 'legal person' is used as an umbrella to identify both natural and artificial persons as the equivalent of a 'legal subject' or a 'subject of the law' (P), that is, the centre of a 'right' or 'rights'.[52] However, it is preferable to refer more simply to the concept of a 'person' to identify a 'subject' of claims, obligations, rights and duties because the concept of a 'legal person' is more often used to single out artificial subjects of claims, obligations, rights and duties.[53]

Contrary to individuals, who can act and speak in order to exercise power, legal persons can only exercise their legal competence via designated organs (LP_{Pcomp}), which are individuals entrusted to exercise power on their behalf.[54] Within national legal orders, all natural and legal persons have, in principle, legal competence (P_{comp}), although this can be diminished or excluded under specific circumstances: for instance, as concerns children and incapacitated persons. Indeed, legal competence is subject to age and rationality conditions, fundamentally corresponding to those of an adult of sound mind.[55] In this context, individuals, NGOs and corporations can only act on a private basis through contractual power $\left(P_{pow \rightarrow contract \leftarrow pow}P\right)$, thus creating, varying and removing claims, obligations, rights and duties under 'private' law. Besides

45 Kelsen, *Reine Rechtslehre* (*Pure Theory*), 1934, at 148–149; Kurki, *A Theory*, 2019, at 9.
46 Kurki, *A Theory*, 2019, at 94.
47 K. Tuori, *Critical Legal Positivism*, Ashgate, 2002, at 186.
48 S.M. Wise, 'Legal Personhood and the Nonhuman Rights Project' (2010) 17 *Animal Law Review* 1, at 5.
49 Kurki, *A Theory*, 2019, at 8.
50 Kelsen, *Reine Rechtslehre* (*Pure Theory*), 1934, at 174.
51 Kurki, *A Theory*, 2019, at 7.
52 Kurki, *A Theory*, 2019, at 7.
53 See, for instance, Kurki, *A Theory*, 2019, at 1 ff.
54 Kelsen, *Reine Rechtslehre* (*Pure Theory*), 1934, at 177.
55 See Kurki, *A Theory*, 2019, at 10.

exercising contractual power $\left(St_{Ppow \rightarrow contract \leftarrow pow} P\right)$, States can exercise 'public' sovereign power—that is, competence—unilaterally to create, vary and remove rights and duties, notably through acts of government $\left(St_{Gov \rightarrow law\text{-}making}\right)$ under 'public' law.

1.4 Sphere of validity of a norm: space and time

A norm has a specific sphere of validity, which is defined by both space (4) and time (5). These are indeed the elements that outline the limits of normative effectiveness, in light of the fact that human conduct takes place in a given space at a specified time.[56] In the same way that we need three spatial coordinates and a temporal one to represent physical phenomena,[57] spatial and temporal coordinates are necessary to outline the validity of the law.

First, norms have defined validity in space (4 (sp)), which means they have a specific territorial sphere (•) of application.[58] Such a territorial sphere of validity is primarily determined by the concept of a State, simply because the globe is divided spatially among nation-states, which exercise equal sovereign power over territories delimited by borders.[59] Accordingly, in *S.S. Lotus*, the Permanent Court of International Justice (PCIJ) held that 'jurisdiction is certainly territorial'.[60] A territory indeed delimits the validity of State normative power in space, as clearly pointed out by the Arbitral Tribunal in *Island of Palmas*: '[s]overeignty in relation to a portion of the surface of the globe is the legal condition necessary for the inclusion of such portion in the territory of any particular State'.[61]

Second, norms have validity in time (5 (t)).[62] Although we do not precisely know what time is,[63] this concept is a fundamental element for organising societal relationships and is strictly related to the idea of space.[64] Think,

56 See Kelsen, *General Theory*, 1945, at 42; Kelsen, *Allgemeine Theorie der Normen*, 1979, at 144.

57 C. Audoin and B. Guinot, *The Measurement of Time: Time, Frequency and the Atomic Clock*, Cambridge University Press, 2001, at 6 ff.

58 Kelsen, *General Theory*, 1945, at 42; S. Müller-Mall, *Legal Spaces: Towards a Topological Thinking of Law*, Springer, 2013, at 64–65.

59 W.C. Dimock, 'Time against Territoriality: National Laws and Literary Translations', in A. Sarat, L. Douglas and M.M. Umphrey (eds.), *The Place of Law*, The University of Michigan Press, 2009, 21, at 22.

60 *S.S. Lotus (France v. Turkey)* [1927] PCIJ Ser. A No. 10, 4, at 18.

61 *Island of Palmas (Netherlands v. U.S.)*, Award of 4 April 1928 (1928) II *Reports of International Arbitral Awards* 829, at 838.

62 See Kelsen, *Allgemeine Theorie*, 1979, at 144–146.

63 A. Wilschut, *Images of Time: The Role of a Historical Consciousness of Time in Learning History*, IAP, 2012, at 33 ff.

64 See T. Maudlin, *Philosophy of Physics: Space and Time*, Princeton University Press, 2012, at 117; O. Pooley, 'Space and Time', in Curd and Psillos (eds.), *The Routledge Companion*, 2014, 507.

for instance, that time was initially measured based on the position of the Sun.[65] More fundamentally, through coordinated universal time (UTC),[66] legal relationships are first and foremost organised based on a division of the globe into 'meridians', at least, since 200 BCE, that is, lines of longitude defining time-zones (terrestrial time) running between the North and South Poles, whereby the prime meridian (standard of time or Greenwich time) was determined to pass at Greenwich by the resolutions of the International Meridian Conference held in Washington, DC, in 1884, involving an antemeridian at 180° longitude identifying the international date line.[67] Within this general timeframe, more detailed timeframes are set within and outside the State. Thus, domestic and international legal relationships can come into existence temporally by means of entering a contract for sale of goods, but these extinguish when possession of the goods is effectively transmitted to the buyer, who fulfils the obligation to pay a price $(t_1 \rightarrow t_2)$.[68] More fundamentally, a State can come into existence and extinguish under specific circumstances, which means that the rights and duties it entails have limited validity in time $(t_1 \rightarrow t_2)$,[69] ultimately based on the exercise of the right to self-determination of peoples. In this regard, scholars speak of 'momentary legal systems' and the 'birth' and 'death' of a State.[70] Thus, for instance, the State of Zanzibar was created in 1963 and extinguished in 1965. For a State to come into existence, it needs to acquire title to territorial sovereignty,[71] which happens by means such as occupation (of *terra nullius*), prescription (of sovereignty), cession, transfer and conquest (of a sovereign territory).[72] By contrast, a State ceases to exist when one or more constitutive elements—notably, governmental authority, territory or population—are missing. Thus, for example, Tanganyika and Zanzibar ceased to exist by merging into Tanzania in

65 D. McCarthy and P.K. Seidelmann, *Time: From Earth Rotation to Atomic Physics*, Cambridge University Press, 2018, 2nd ed., at 262 ff.

66 McCarthy and Seidelmann, *Time*, 2018, at 249.

67 J. Levine, 'GPS and the Legal Traceability of Time' (2001) *GPS World* 52, at 60; K. Birth, 'Standards in the Shadows for Everyone to See: The Supranational Regulation of Time and the Concern over Temporal Pluralism', in S. Beynon-Jones and E. Grabham (eds.), *Law and Time*, Routledge, 2019, 106, at 202 ff.; McCarthy and Seidelmann, *Time*, 2018, at 10 ff. and 334 ff.

68 See R.E. Barnett, 'Contract Is Not a Promise; Contract Is Consent', in G. Klass, G. Letsas and P. Saprai (eds.), *Philosophical Foundations of Contract Law*, Oxford University Press, 2014, 41, at 49; E. Bulygin, 'Time and Validity', in C. Bernal, C. Huerta, T. Mazzarese, J.J. Moreso, P.E. Navarro and S.L. Paulson (eds.), *Essays in Legal Philosophy*, Oxford University Press, 2015, 171, at 174.

69 Kelsen, *General Theory*, 1945, at 218; D. Christian, *Maps of Time: An Introduction to Big History*, 2004, University of California Press.

70 Kelsen, *General Theory*, 1945, at 219; J. Raz, *The Concept of a Legal System*, Clarendon Press, 1980, at 187.

71 *Frontier Dispute (Burkina Faso v. Republic of Mali) (Judgment)* [1986] ICJ Reports 554, at 586, para. 63.

72 See, for instance, Kelsen, *General Theory*, 1945, at 213–216.

1964, while the Union of Soviet Socialist Republics (USSR) was extinguished by dismemberment in 1991, with the Russian Federation successfully claiming continuation. Sometimes, extinction materialises via negotiation. Thus, for example, the Polish-Lithuanian Commonwealth dissolved into Poland and Lithuania under the Treaty of Versailles in 1919.

1.5 Formalising legal concepts (legal geometries): the deontic network

Ultimately, the foundation of every legal construction is the claim—obligation (or obligation—claim) relationship,[73] and a norm can be thought of on the basis of five axiomatic elements (necessary and sufficient conditions). In fact, a norm can be conceived of as a (sum of) claim—obligation (or right—duty) relationship(s) (1) that regulate(s) conduct (action or inaction) (2) among persons (3) in a defined space (4) and time (5) $\left(\mathrm{P}_{1,2\ldots\ \mathrm{claim(right)} \rightarrow \mathrm{(no)\,act} - \mathrm{act(no)} \leftarrow \mathrm{(duty)\,obl} \ldots 4,3}\,\mathrm{P}_{(\mathrm{sp/t})}\right)$.

This can be expressed concisely via Kripke-style symbolic notation.

$$\textbf{\textit{Norm}} =_{\mathrm{p1,(p2)}} \textbf{\textit{Claim(Right)}}\,\mathrm{(NON)A{-}(NON)A}\textbf{\textit{Obl}}(\textbf{\textit{Duty}})_{\mathrm{p3,(p4)\,space/time}}$$

The word 'right' ('*Recht*', '*droit*', '*diritto*', '*derecho*', '*direito*') comes from the Latin term '*directum*', which is the past participle of the verb '*dirigere*' and means 'to line up', 'to trace a certain direction', and thus, 'to set out, to set in order, to regulate, to rule': it indicates what is in a straight line as opposed to what is tortuous. Such a feature is spontaneously attributed to a ruler, which is used to trace straight lines, so much so that one can visualise formally the idea of a right—duty relationship as a link among persons.[74] Thus, the law (as a set of rights), can be considered to trace an ideal line among persons that outlines their conduct as precisely as possible (P—P).

In light of Peirce's triadic theory of the sign, including likenesses (icons), indications and symbols,[75] it is possible to formulate an iconic representation of minimum necessary legal notions, thus moving from a language of words into a language of forms. In fact, icons convey reality by way of imitation (resemblance) and are thus likenesses of their objects; in other words, they are suggestive and possess the signified quality by completely substituting the object.[76] Notably, geometrical figures are fundamentally instances of their

73 See Drago, 'La notion d'obligation' (2000) at 44.

74 See Sériaux, *Le droit: une introduction*, 1997, at 19 and 24 ff.

75 Peirce, 'What Is a Sign?', 1894, at 5–10.

76 C.S. Peirce, 'On the Algebra of Logic: A Contribution to the Philosophy of Notation, 1880', in N. Houser and C.J.W. Kloesel (eds.), *The Essential Peirce*, Indiana University Press, Vol. I, 1992, 225, at 226; Peirce, 'Of Reasoning in General', 1895, Peirce, Vol. II, 1998, 11, at 13; Peirce, 'New Elements (*Καινὰ στοιχεία*)', 1904, Peirce, 300, at 307.

objects. By contrast, indications, such as a signpost, show something about things; in other words, they are imperative and in real reaction with the object denoted.[77] Symbols, in turn, including words and phrases, describe things; in other words, they are indicative and determine the interpretant sign.[78]

Based on likenesses, it is it possible to convey and 'map' the law as a system of icons. This approach simplifies legal reasoning because icons are straightforward in predicating qualities.[79] By positing the view that the law is a system of iconic signs, the idea is creating a '(neural) network'[80] so as to achieve a synthetic and therefore unitary mental representation of the legal system(s). It has indeed been acknowledged that, from the standpoint of legal semiotics, Peirce's methodology approaching semantics as a triadic sign system can be relied on to account for structures of legal reasoning, understanding his theory of the 'sign' as a theory of the 'legal sign'.[81] Within this framework, the intuitive idea is specifically moving from a description of legal concepts by way of linguistic signs to a merely iconic representation of legal notions.[82] By commencing with a very simple iconic representation of fundamental legal concepts, it is possible to elaborate a complex image of the legal order, based on 'simple and easy long chains of reasoning'.[83] As a result, the legal system can be represented as a 'machine', and the law appears as 'social geometry', providing a visual logical representation of societal reality whereby it can be asserted that legal logic, as normative logic, is formal logic: *law is form*.

The idea is formalising core theoretical legal tools through iconic likenesses, particularly the fundamental deontic modalities of claim, obligation, right and duty, which can be regarded as an application of (social) network theory to fundamental deontic concepts. The concept of a 'network' is relational and very powerful. A network can be defined as a system encompassing many similar parts that are connected in order to allow movement or

77 Peirce, 'What Is a Sign?', 1894, at 5; Peirce, 'New Elements', in N. Houser and C.J.W. Kloesel (eds.), *The Essential Peirce*, 1998, at 307.

78 Peirce, 'New Elements', 1904 at 307.

79 Peirce, 'Of Reasoning', 1895, at 17.

80 See J.A. Freeman, *Simulating Neural Networks with Mathematica*, Addison-Wesley, 1994, at 6–7; H. Abdi, D. Valentin and B. Edelman, *Neural Networks*, Sage University Press, 1999, at 1; A.S. d'Avila Garcez, K.B. Broda and D.M. Gabbay (eds.), *Neural-Symbolic Learning Systems: Foundations and Applications*, Springer, 2002; M. Newman, A.-L. Barabási and D.J. Watts (eds.), *The Structure and Dynamics of Networks*, Princeton University Press, 2006; M. Newman, *Networks: An Introduction*, Oxford University Press, 2010, at 36 ff.

81 Kevelson, *The Law as a System*, 1988, at 4, 12 and 15.

82 See further A.C.R. van Riel and C. Horvath, 'Conceptualizing Intuition as a Mental Faculty: Towards a "Critique of Intuitive Reason" and a Process Model of Intuition', in M. Sinclair (ed.), *Handbook of Research Methods on Intuition*, Edward Elgar, 2014, 42, at 46–47.

83 Descartes, *Discours*, 1637, at II.

communication between or along the parts or between the parts and a control centre.[84] Network theory is an area of applied and network science, as well as part of graph theory, and concerns many disciplines, including particle physics, computer science, biology, economics and sociology.[85] The fundamental difference between a non-network explanation of a phenomenon and a network interpretation is the inclusion of concepts and information on relationships in a study: network analysis elaborates structures in terms of networks of linkages among units. Examples of network analysis encompass logistical networks, the World Wide Web, gene regulatory networks, metabolic networks, epistemological networks and sociological networks.[86] Network theory largely exploits diagrams to represent relationships between discrete objects and provides new ways for answering research questions through a precise formal definition of scientific problems.[87]

As a branch of network theory, social network analysis is a relatively new technique. It focuses on relationships among interacting social units, which are often visualised so as to be systematically understood as structures.[88] Social network analysis is useful for investigating various types of relationships, such as kinship patterns, community structures and interlocking directorships.[89] It is an inherently interdisciplinary attempt, and its concepts have been developed out of the concurrence of social theory with formal mathematical, statistical and computing methodology.[90] The central concepts of 'relationship', 'network' and 'structure' have arisen almost independently in several social and behavioural disciplines, starting with the structural concerns of the anthropologist Radcliffe-Brown to later involve sociologists.[91] Basically, social network analysis is concerned with understanding the linkages among social entities and their implications.[92] From the viewpoint of social network analysis, the social environment can be conceptualised via patterns (structures) of regularities in relationships among interacting units. The social network perspective encompasses theories, models and applications that are expressed in terms of relational concepts or processes, whereby the

84 D. Knoke and J.H. Kulinski, *Network Analysis*, Sage, 1982, at 12; K. Erciyes, *Complex Networks: An Algorithmic Perspective*, CRC, 2015, at 1.

85 Newman, Barabási and Watts, *The Structure and Dynamics*, 2006, at 1; Newmann, *Networks: An Introduction*, 2010, at 1.

86 Newmann, *Networks*, 2010, at 3 ff.

87 Newman, Barabási and Watts, *The Structure and Dynamics*, 2006, at 3; Newmann, *Networks*, 2010, at 37 ff.

88 C. Prell and D.R. Schaefer, 'An Introduction to Social Network Analysis', in J. McLevey, J. Scott and P.J. Carrington (eds.), *The Sage Handbook of Social Network Analysis*, Sage, 2024, 19, at 20.

89 Erciyes, *Complex Networks*, 2015, at 3 and 227.

90 Erciyes, *Complex Networks*, 2015, at 19–20.

91 Erciyes, *Complex Networks*, 2015, at 19–20.

92 Erciyes, *Complex Networks*, 2015, at 19–20.

fundamental blocks include relationships conveyed by linkages among units. Within network models, societies are conceived of as webs of linkages among units and regularities (patterns) in interaction give rise to structures. The social network environment thus focuses on entities involving a collection of individuals and their reciprocal linkages, constraining action.[93] Social network theory makes liberal use of three types of notation: graph-theoretic notation, sociometric notation, and algebraic notation, whereby graph-theoretic notation can be seen as an elementary way to represent actors and their relationships.[94]

In sum, social network analysis is grounded in structural concerns about 'interweaving' and 'interlocking' relationships through which social patterns are organised via textile-based metaphors such as the 'fabric' and 'web' of societal life.[95] More specifically, network analysis approaches social relationships as 'nodes' (points) and 'ties' (lines), which are visualised through graph-based structures,[96] whereby nodes (•) are the actors within the network and ties (—) identify relationships between the actors.[97] Thus, graphs—a branch of mathematics—allow the visualisation of social networks and matrixes, describing regularities in the patterns of relationships among people (sociograms).[98] In this regard, it is remarkable that graphs and diagrams are conceived of as likenesses in Peirce's theory of the sign.[99]

Graph-theoretic notation for social network analysis might represent, for instance, information received by a job seeker in his or her inner or outer social circles, flows of knowledge, mobilisation of collective action by social movements, institutional policy or dark networks for terrorist campaigns, rather than the relationship between mental health and social support networks.[100]

93 See S. Wasserman and K. Faust, *Social Network Analysis: Methods and Applications*, Cambridge University Press, 1999; J. Scott, *Social Network Analysis*, Sage, 2017.

94 D. Knoke and S. Yang, *Social Network Analysis*, Sage, 2020, at 56 ff.

95 Scott, *Social Network Analysis*, 2017, at 2; Knoke and Yang, *Social Network Analysis*, 2020, at 7.

96 See C. Chen, W. Härdle and A. Unwin, *Handbook on Data Visualization*, Springer, 2008; J. Bender and M. Marrinan, *The Culture of Diagram*, Stanford University Press, 2010, at 47–51; A. Kirk, *Data Visualisation: A Handbook for Data Driven Design*, Sage, 2016.

97 Scott, *Social Network Analysis*, 2017, at 75.

98 C. Prell, *Social Network Analysis*, Sage, 2012, at 9–10; Knoke and Yang, *Social Network Analysis*, 2020, at 8.

99 Peirce, 'Of Reasoning', 1895, at 13.

100 Newmann, *Networks*, 2010, at 37; Knoke and Yang, *Social Network Analysis*, 2020, at 9; C. Prell, and D.R. Schaefer, *Introducing Social Network Analysis*, Sage, 2024, at 19. See further E. Estrada, *The Structure of Complex Networks: Theory and Applications*, Oxford University Press, 2012, at 6 ff.; C. Lee, 'The Game of Go: Bounded Rationality and Artificial Intelligence', in E. Elliot and L.D. Kiel (eds.), *Complex Systems in the Social and Behavioural Sciences: Theory, Methods and Application*, University of Michigan Press, 2021, 157, at 166; M. Diani, 'Political and Policy Networks', in McLevey, Scott and Carrington (eds.), *The Sage Handbook*, 2024, 130; C. Prell, J. Hollway, P. Matous and Y. Todo, 'International Trade Networks', ibid., at 350.

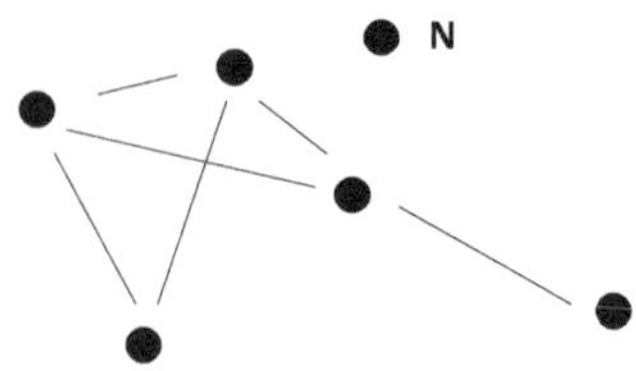

Figure 1.1 Social network: nodes and ties (sociogram)

Based on nodes and ties, graph-theoretic representation can be notated as $n_1 \neq n_2, n_3 \rightarrow n_4$, and so on, whereby the qualities of the network can be roughly divided into two categories: attribute data and relational data.[101] Attribute data concern qualities of the agents (nodes), such as opinions, and thus identify the features of the nodes. On the other hand, relational data, such as financial exchanges, are the ties that establish a relationship between one agent and another, whereby relationships connect agents into larger relational systems, and relational data are especially important to the concerns of the social tradition because they simplify and highlight the structure of social action. Within this framework, fundamental concepts include the elements of an 'actor', 'relational tie', 'dyad', 'triad', 'group', 'subgroup' and 'network'.[102] Thus, 'actors' are social entities and therefore discrete, individual and collective social units. A 'relational tie' can have different content but necessarily entails a linkage between a pair of actors. A 'dyad' is a linkage between two actors while a 'triad' is a subset of three actors and associated ties. A 'group' involves the collection of a finite set of actors linked by specific theoretical or empirical reasons, whereas 'subgroup' defines any subset of actors and all ties among them. A 'network' identifies a set of ties of a specific type among all the members of a group; thus, a 'social network' includes a finite set or sets of actors and their reciprocal relationship(s).[103]

As network analysis is useful in the area of sciences in general and is also relevant to social sciences, it is arguably applicable to the law and all of its branches; given that it is concerned with societal regulation,[104] a network approach to the law should be possible. Indeed, as network analysis is particularly interested in relational sociology,[105] notably in the structural features of social relationships between individuals and groups,[106] it can arguably also

101 Knoke and Yang, *Social Network Analysis*, 2020, at 10 ff.

102 Knoke and Yang, *Social Network Analysis*, 2020, at 11 ff.

103 Prell and Schaefer, 'An Introduction', 2023, at 21.

104 Newmann, *Networks*, 2010, at 36 ff.

105 Scott, *Social Network Analysis*, 2017, at 8. On relational sociology, see N. Luhmann, *Die Gesellschaft der Gesellschaft (Theory of Society)*, 1997, Suhrkamp, tr. R. Barrett, Stanford University Press, 2013, Vol. I, at 1.

106 Scott, *Social Network Analysis*, 2017, at 73; Knoke and Yang, *Social Network Analysis*, 2020, at 7.

apply to legal relationships, which are part of the sociological construct.[107] Key concepts overlap, given that social network analysis deals with 'interactions', 'relationships' and 'networks', including individual natural persons, small groups, organisations and even nation-states.[108] The idea is therefore elaborating a network approach to the law within the broader field of social network analysis. Against this background, according to deontic logic, the law can be conceived of as a set of rules—or duties—governing human conduct.[109] Combining deontic logic and social network analysis, particularly through graph-theoretic notation, discloses a formal model of the law revolving around the correlated notions of 'claim', 'obligation', 'right' and 'duty', regarded as formal 'ties' (—), among 'persons' (P), regarded as 'nodes' (•). Within this framework, deontic concepts are formalised via network theory and legal knowledge emerges as a synthetic formal network, notably as a formalised deontic network, outlining a formal network theory of the law.

Naturally, the law involves specific techniques: it differs from other social sciences and can furthermore be approached in different ways. Thus, applying network theory to the law from an ontological, deontological or sociological perspective presumably leads to different outcomes. All these applications deserve to be developed and can lead to interesting results. As our analysis is confined to legal ontology and relies on a few simplified legal tools provided by deontic logic in order to explain the law as 'it is' in its positivistic dimension, the ultimate idea is applying basic network theory to fundamental deontic concepts. Indeed, the building blocks of deontic logic—that is, the concepts of a 'permission', 'obligation', 'right' and 'duty'—are relational notions. Given that the distinguishing feature of (social) network theory is the exploration of concepts and information on relationships,[110] it is possible to regard deontic concepts as structures conceived of in terms of network linkages between units. On this basis, the various notations of social network theory can apply to deontic logic, and, by relying on graph-theoretic notation, it is possible to visualise deontic entities, translating Kripke-style semantics into graph-theoretic notation (sociograms). As a consequence, a visual network of deontic relationships emerges, mapping the law as a deontic system (P—P).

Developing a formal representation of minimum deontic concepts in terms of nodes and ties allows a movement from natural language and Kripke-style semantics into a language of graphic forms, which describe reality by way of imitation and thus make it possible to 'map' the law as an iconic system. The

107 A. Giddens, *The Constitution of Society*, Polity Press, 1984, at 16 ff.; L.J. McIntyre, *Law in the Sociological Enterprise*, Westview Press, 1994, at 31–46; K. McGee and B. Latour, *The Normativity of Networks*, Routledge, 2014, at 220.

108 Knoke and Yang, *Social Network Analysis*, 2020, at 8.

109 See Sartor, *Legal Reasoning*, 2007, at 453 ff.

110 Sartor, *Legal Reasoning*, 2007, at 453 ff.

idea is outlining a '(neural) network' for achieving a synthetic and therefore comprehensive representation of the legal system(s), thus eventually simplifying and accelerating legal thinking. Concretely, it is as if, rather than describing the pathway to go from Heathrow to the National Gallery in London by means of words, we simply visualise the route on a map. Building on the parallel with the field of art, the analysis follows a minimalistic (ABC) approach, to the extent that it focuses on essential geometrical shapes.[111] Thus, elaborating a very simple representation of basic deontic concepts as nodes and ties leads to developing a systemic and complex image of the legal order(s). As a result, legal systems appear as 'machines', and the law unfolds as (Euclidean) 'social geometry', affording a logical visual representation of societal reality. In this sense, it is possible to assume that the logic of the law—or normative logic—is formal logic and to conclude that the law is form.

On this basis, in graph-theoretic notation, the correlated notions of 'claim' and 'obligation' can be represented as 'ties' and, therefore, 'lines' (—) linking persons (P), which can in turn be visualised as 'nodes' (•). Thus, it is possible to develop a graph-theoretic visualisation of Kripke-style normative formulas, which are nothing other than simple social matrixes, through sociograms. In the context of an ontological analysis of the law, the purpose is not so much achieving a graphic representation of statistical quantitative and qualitative aspects of societal relationships[112] as outlining a graphic visualisation of legal relationships as such (as a sub-domain of social relationships),[113] in order to facilitate a mapping of the legal system and, thus, a simple comprehension of legal mechanics through 'semantic frames'.[114]

Thus, the normative formula (social matrix) $\boldsymbol{Claim}_{p1}$(NON)A—$\boldsymbol{Obl}_{p2}$ (NON)A $\left(P_{1\ \text{claim}\rightarrow(\text{no})\text{act}\leftarrow\text{obl}}P_2\right)$ can be visualised through iconic graph-theoretic notation.

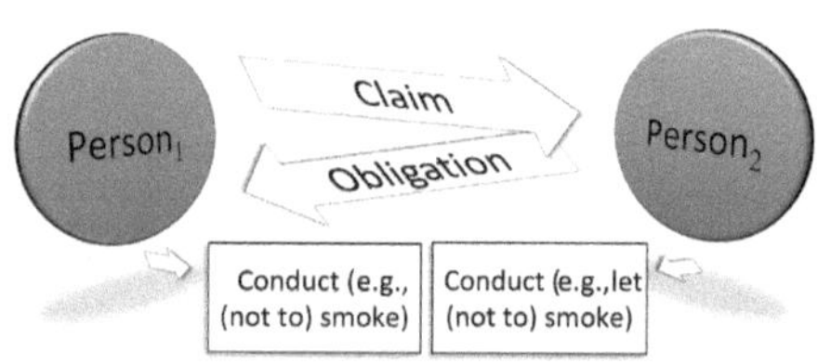

Figure 1.2 Claim—Obligation $\left(P_{1\ \text{claim}\rightarrow(\text{no})\ \text{act}\leftarrow\text{obl}}P_2\right)$

111 Fried, 'Art and Objecthood' (1967) at 12–13.

112 See, for instance, K. Namboodiri, *Matrix Algebra: An Introduction*, Sage, 1984; T.A.B. Snijders and R.J. Bosker, *Multilevel Analysis: An Introduction to Basic and Advanced Multilevel Modeling*, Sage, 2003; K. Healy, *Data Visualization*, Princeton University Press, 2019.

113 Prell, *Social Network Analysis*, 2012, at 10.

114 Y. Zhang and Z. Teng, *Natural Language Processing: A Machine Learning Perspective*, Cambridge University Press, 2021, at 11–12; A. Negro, *Graph-Powered Machine Learning*, Manning Publications, 2021, at 18.

In this framework, nodes (•) represent persons, whereas the linking tie-lines outline a claim—obligation (or obligation—claim) relationship governing conduct (action or inaction: $P_{\rightarrow(\text{no})\text{act}}$) between persons, providing a simple graphic representation of a bilateral norm $(P_1 - P_2)$.

Along these lines, the normative formula of a right $\left(\boldsymbol{Right}_{\text{p1}}(\text{NON})\text{A} - \boldsymbol{Obl}_{\text{p2,p3}}(\text{NON})\text{A}\left(P_{1\ \text{right}\rightarrow(\text{no})\ \text{act}\leftarrow\text{obl}}P_{2,3}\right)\right)$ can also be visualised through graph-theoretic notation (figure 1.3).

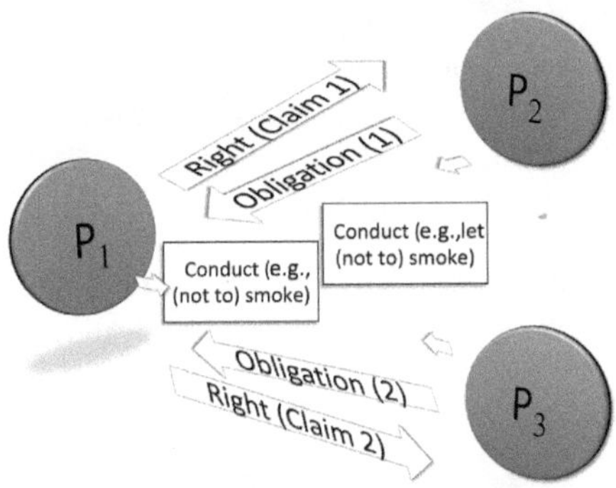

Figure 1.3 Right—Obligations $\left(P_{1\ \text{right}\rightarrow(\text{no})\text{act}\leftarrow\text{obl}}P_{2,3}\right)$

In this context, the linking tie-lines represent claim—obligation relationships, the sum of which outlines a right for a person (P_1) vis-à-vis two other persons (P_2 and P_3).

Correspondingly, the normative formula of a duty $\left(\boldsymbol{Duty}_{\text{p1}}(\text{NON})\text{A} - \boldsymbol{Claim}_{\text{p2,p3}}(\text{NON})\text{A}\left(P_{1\ \text{duty}\rightarrow(\text{no})\ \text{act}\leftarrow\text{claim}}P_{2,3}\right)\right)$ can be visualised through graph-theoretic notation (figure 1.4).

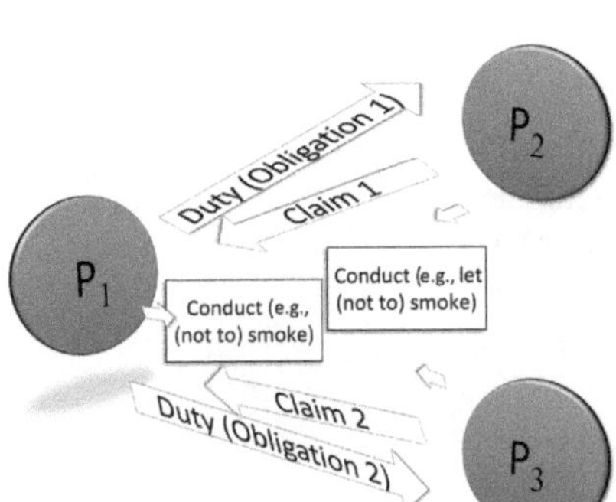

Figure 1.4 Duty—Claims $\left(P_{1\ \text{duty}\rightarrow(\text{no})\text{act}\leftarrow\text{claim}}P_{2,3}\right)$

In this context, the linking tie-lines represent obligation—claim relationships, the sum of which outlines a duty for a person (P_1) vis-à-vis two other persons (P_2 and P_3).

Within this framework, it is interesting to observe that there is complete correlativeness not only between claims and obligations but also between rights and duties $\left(P_{1,2\ldots claim(right)\rightarrow(no)act\leftarrow(duty)\ obl}P_{3,4\ldots}\right)$.

$$\boldsymbol{Righ}_{p1}(\text{NON})\text{A} - \boldsymbol{Obl}_{p2,p3}(\text{NON})\text{A}$$
$$\boldsymbol{Right}_{p2}(\text{NON})\text{A} - \boldsymbol{Obl}_{p1,p3}(\text{NON})\text{A}$$
$$\boldsymbol{Right}_{p3}(\text{NON})\text{A} - \boldsymbol{Obl}_{p1,p2}(\text{NON})\text{A}$$
$$\boldsymbol{Claim}_{p2,p3}(\text{NON})\text{A} - \boldsymbol{Duty}_{p1}(\text{NON})\text{A}$$
$$\boldsymbol{Claim}_{p1,p3}(\text{NON})\text{A} - \boldsymbol{Duty}_{p2}(\text{NON})\text{A}$$
$$\boldsymbol{Claim}_{p1,p2}(\text{NON})\text{A} - \boldsymbol{Duty}_{p3}(\text{NON})\text{A}$$

Such a Kripke-style semantic matrix can be visualised through graph-theoretic notation (figure 1.5).

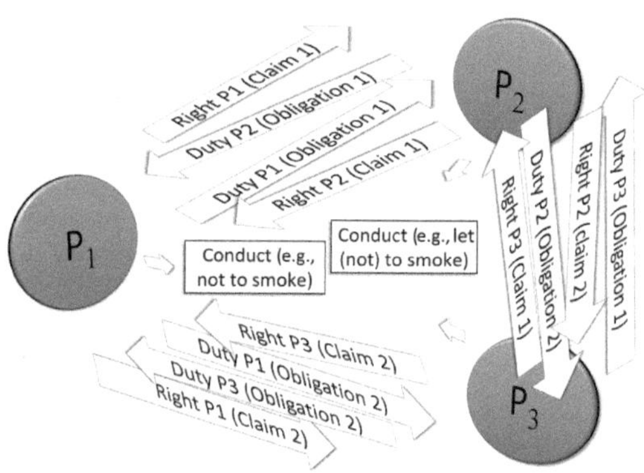

Figure 1.5 Right—Duty $\left(P_{1,2\ldots claim(right)\rightarrow(no)act\leftarrow(duty)obl}P_{3,4\ldots}\right)$

In this sense, it is possible to affirm that 'the right of one is always the obligation of another' and 'right and obligation can never be isolated from each other'.[115]

115 Kelsen, *Reine Rechtslehre (Introduction)*, 1934, at 51.

2 Normative systems

2.1 Rights and duties (norms)

Norms do not exist alone except for the two merely hypothetical legal systems in which any conduct is permitted—that is, negative society, according to Bentham,[1] or the peaceful 'law of nature' outlined by Rousseau rather than the Hobbesian '*bellum omnium contra omnes*'[2]—and the opposite where any conduct is prohibited. These systems are necessarily theoretical as they are intrinsically inconsistent, given that they would allow and prohibit, for instance, the right to property at the same time. Such 'mono-normative' systems constitute the opposite extremes of a spectrum where two or more norms combine with one another to establish a legal order and constrain freedom to a lesser or broader extent.[3] Within the spectrum, prompted by the need for self-preservation rather than universal rationality, *res publica* can be taxonomised according to different political schemes such as monarchy, aristocracy and democracy,[4] between the extremes of anarchy and totalitarianism.[5] When

1 J. Bentham, *A Fragment on Government*, 1776, Cambridge University Press, 1988, at 40.

2 J.J. Rousseau, *Discours sur l'origine et les fondements de l'inégalité parmi les hommes*, M.M. Rey, 1755; T. Hobbes, *Leviathan*, 1651, ed. N. Malcolm, Clarendon Press, 2012, Vol. 2, at 254. See further J. Locke, *Two Treatises of Government*, 1690, C. Baldwin, 1824, at 130 ff.

3 See T. Moore, *Utopia*, 1513, tr. D. Baker-Smith, Penguin, 2012; Kant, 'Die Metaphysik der Sitten', 1997, at 94 ff.; F. Hayek, *The Constitution of Liberty*, 1960, Routledge, reprinted 2008, at 130; E. Levinas, 'Liberté et commandement' (1953) 58(3) *Revue de Métaphysique et de Morale* 264; N. Holtung and K. Lippert-Rasmussen (eds.), *Egalitarianism: New Essays on the Nature and Value of Equality*, Oxford University Press, 2007.

4 N. Machiavelli, *De Principatibus (The Prince)*, 1513, tr. T. Parks, Penguin, 2009, at 5 ff.; J. Bodin, *Les six livres de la République*, Jacques du Puys, 1576; B. Spinoza, *Tractatus Politicus (Political Treatise)*, 1676, Hackett, 2000; J.J. Rousseau, *Du contrat social, ou principes du droit politique*, M.M. Rey, 1762; Kant, 'Die Metaphysik der Sitten', 1997, at 83 ff.; B. Russell, *Power: A New Social Analysis*, Allen and Unwin Ltd., 1938, at 188; F. Fukuyama, *The End of History and the Last Man*, Free Press, 1992.

5 K. Marx, 'Economic and Philosophical Manuscripts', 1844, in D. McLellan (ed.), *Marx: Selected Writings*, Oxford University Press, 1977, at 75; F. Nietzsche, *Menschliches, Allzumenschliches: Ein Buch für freie Geister (Human, All Too Human: A Book for Free Spirits)*, 1878,

DOI: 10.4324/9781003228318-3

several norms interact, entering into relationships with one another, a normative system comes into being,[6] and we move from the study of a norm as the elementary unit of legal logic to the analysis of norms aggregated into legal systems (orders).[7] Given that mono-normative legal systems are purely hypothetical, it can be safely considered that the law is a normative system, including a plurality of rules that are organised into a unity.[8] Such a unity covers all human conduct, which is regulated either explicitly or implicitly, assuming that behaviour that is not explicitly prohibited is (implicitly) permitted.[9]

The fact that norms can combine systemically entails that they are interrelated and constitute organised systems. By considering that a norm outlines a claim—obligation (or obligation—claim) or right—duty (or duty—right) relationship (P—P) that regulates conduct (action or inaction) among persons $\left(P_{\rightarrow(\text{no})\text{act}}\right)$,[10] a normative system can be consistently seen as an ordered set of claim—obligation (or obligation—claim) and right—duty (or duty—right) relationships—that is, a deontic network—that regulates conduct (action or inaction) among persons in given space and time $\left(P_{1,2\ldots\rightarrow(\text{no})\text{act}—\text{act}(\text{no})\leftarrow\ldots4,3}P_{(\text{sp/t})}\right)$. Thus, the totality of the claim—obligation (or obligation—claim) and right—duty (or duty—right) relationships (1) that regulate conduct (action or inaction) (2) among all persons (3) in space (4) and time (5) $\left(P_{1,2\ldots\ \text{claim(right)}\rightarrow(\text{no})\text{act}\leftarrow(\text{duty})\text{obl}}\,P_{3,4\ldots}\right)$ constitutes the legal or 'juridical' system (order): that is, the law, in an objective sense, as an aggregation of subjective legal relationships. Indeed, such a deontic network—or 'legal cosmos'

---

tr. R.J. Hollingdale, Cambridge University Press, 1986, at 162 ff.; C. Schmitt, *Die Diktatur: Von den Anfängen des modernen Souveränitätsgedankens bis zum proletarischen Klassenkampf (The Dictatorship: From the Origin of the Modern Concept of Sovereignty to Proletarian Class Struggle)*, 1921, tr. M. Hoelzel and G. Ward, Polity Press, 2014; R. Marcuse, *One-Dimensional Man: Studies in the Ideology of Advanced Industrial Society*, Beacon Press, 1964; R. Nozick, *Anarchy, State and Utopia*, Basic Books, 1974.

6 Raz, *Practical Reason*, 1970, at 107; R. Alexy, *Law's Ideal Dimension*, Oxford University Press, 2021, at 10.

7 See Kelsen, *Reine Rechtslehre* (*Pure Theory*), 1934, at 31; G. Radbruch, *Einführung in die Rechtswissenschaft*, K.F. Koehler Verlag, 1980, at 12; Raz, *The Concept*, 2003, at 24. See further L. Ferrajoli, 'The Past and Future of the Rule of Law', in P. Costa and D. Zolo (eds.), *The Rule of Law: History, Theory and Criticism*, Springer, 2007, 323; R. Libchaber, *L'ordre juridique et le discours du droit: Essai sur les limites de la connaissance du droit*, LGDJ, 2013, at 193 ff.

8 Austin, *The Province of Jurisprudence*, 1832, at 11; Kelsen, *Reine Rechtslehre (Introduction)*, 1934, at 55; Kelsen, *General Theory*, 1945, at 110; M. Del Mar, 'Philosophical Analysis and Historical Inquiry: Theorizing Normativity, Law and Legal Thought', in M.D. Dubber and C. Thomas (eds.), *The Oxford Handbook of Legal History*, Oxford University Press, 2008, 3, at 8; F. Pirie, *The Rule of Laws: A 4,000-Year Quest to Order the World*, Basic Books, 2021, at 3.

9 Raz, *Practical Reason*, 1970, at 86; Kelsen, *Allgemaine Theorie*, 1979, at 131. See further E. Bulygin, 'The Silence of the Law', in Bernal, et al. (eds.), *Essays*, 2015, 293; E. Bulygin and C.E. Alchurrón, 'Permissory Norms and Normative Systems', ibid., 324, at 325.

10 See s. 1.1 and s. 1.2.

(κόσμος), including the totality of legal rules—is also defined as 'objective law' in order to distinguish it from a 'subjective right' as an individual position.[11] However, the so-called 'objective law' can be seen as nothing other than the aggregation of all subjective rights—including correlated duties—encompassing claims and obligations, whereby there is no dualism between objective and subjective law and rights but rather absolute coincidence: rights and duties combine like numbers in mathematics to constitute complex normative orders. Within such a framework, the idea of a norm as a right—duty (or duty—right) and claim—obligation (or obligation—claim) relationship linking persons in space and time permits reconciling the supposed dichotomy between 'objective law' and 'subjective rights' largely discussed in legal theory,[12] whereby 'subjective rights' are simply subsumed into 'objective law' and therefore define its extension. In other words, norms outline subjective rights and correlated duties encompassing correlated claims and obligations, which identify with objective law and outline it as a deontic network.[13]

It is therefore possible to conceive of not only a norm but also of the law as such based on five simple elements: that is, claim—obligation (or obligation—claim) and right—duty (or duty—right) relationships (1), conduct (action or inaction) (2: $P_{\rightarrow(\mathrm{no})\mathrm{act}}$), persons (3: P), space (4: sp) and time (5: t), regarded as necessary and sufficient conditions for legal reasoning.

In a basic hypothetical legal system, including the norms positing the rights to life, to property and to work, such elementary conditions can be expressed via basic Kripke-style semantic notation (matrix).

Right$_{p1}$ to live – ***Obl***$_{p2,p3}$ to let live
Right$_{p2}$ to enjoy property – ***Obl***$_{p1,p3}$ not to interfere with property
Right$_{p3}$ to (elect to) work – ***Obl***$_{p1,p2}$ to let (elect to) work

Kripke-style semantics can be further visualised through graph-theoretic notation. For the purpose of such notation, based on the coincidence between a legal system and its spatial (sphere of) validity,[14] space can be notated spherically as a 'node' (•) (figure 2.1).[15]

Network graph-theoretic notation simply visualises rights and duties, including claims and obligations, as relationships connecting a person (P: node (•)) to other persons (P, P . . . : nodes (••)), whereby the idea emerges

11 See I. Kant, 'Die Metaphysik der Sitten (The Metaphysics of Morals)', 1797, tr. H.B. Nisbeth, in H. Heiss (ed.), *Kant: Political Writings*, Cambridge University Press, 1991, 131, at 132. On the controversial relationship between a subjective right and objective law, see Kelsen, *Reine Rechtslehre (Introduction)*, 1934, at 37–38.

12 Kelsen, *Reine Rechtslehre (Introduction)*, 1934, at 37–38.

13 Along these lines, see Kelsen, *Reine Rechtslehre (Introduction)*, 1934, at 42.

14 See Kelsen, *General Theory*, 1945, at 42.

15 Sowa, *Knowledge Representation*, 2000, at 111.

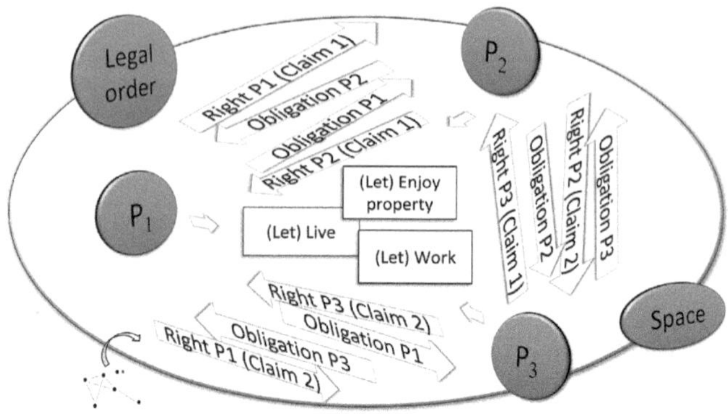

Figure 2.1 Legal system (order) (P—P—P)

that the rights to life, to property and to work are normative connections (ties) between a person (node) and all the other persons (nodes) of a legal system, entailing correlated duties not to interfere with the enjoyment and disposal of specific values and things (P—P—P).[16]

2.2 (Normative) conduct in time (the law clock): procedure(s)

Norms are specifically connected through procedures, which are the means to create, vary, remove and enforce rules (claims, obligations, rights and duties: P—P), whereby the law governs its own regulation.[17] A 'procedure' can be defined as a sequence of active or inactive conduct (action and inaction: $\left(P_{\rightarrow(\text{no})\text{act}\rightarrow}P_{\rightarrow(\text{no})\text{act}}\right)$ performed in a specific time lapse ($t \rightarrow t$: interval or set of instants). In fact, although we do not exactly know what it is, time is defined, inter alia, as a 'measured or measurable period during which an action, process, or condition exists or continues'.[18]

While the importance of procedures as a key element of legal logic has been envisaged by scholars working on legal semiotics,[19] surprisingly, there is no exhaustive work on legal procedures per se in scholarly research. There is rather work that, following a sectoral approach, identifies legal procedures with the judiciary.[20] Perhaps even more surprisingly, the concept of 'time'

16 Kelsen, *Reine Rechtslehre (Introduction)*, 1934, at 42.
17 Kelsen, *Reine Rechtslehre (Introduction)*, 1934, at 132.
18 G. Merriam, C. Merriam and N. Webster, 'Time', https://www.merriam-webster.com/dictionary/time.
19 See Kevelson, *The Law as a System*, 1988, at 7.
20 See, for instance, J. Collier and V. Lowe, *The Settlement of Disputes in International Law: Institutions and Procedures*, Oxford University Press, 1999; K. Lenaerts, *EU Procedural Law*, Oxford University Press, 2nd ed., 2023.

has been scarcely studied in the legal field and writings on the issue can be essentially counted on the fingers of one hand.[21] As time and its structure have gone largely ignored in the legal field, it is interesting to consider the forms and functioning of the legal horology and to explore its patterns, turns and chronography. Neither has the link between time and procedure been given extensive attention.

The history of calendars covers practices with archaic roots: people created various methods for tracking divisions of time for purposes often connected to religious, astronomic and agricultural praxis. Archaeologists have indeed unveiled timekeeping methods that go back to prehistoric times at least as old as Neolithic societies, with calendars used as timekeeping schemes based on the day, the solar year and lunation (natural clocks).[22] The Sumerian, Egyptian and Assyrian calendars have become famous.[23] Within the larger time lapse outlined by calendars, clever artisans and factors built the oldest clocks predominantly for the Church, with trailblazing timepieces measuring passing hours in cathedral halls (man-made clocks),[24] whereby the church—a centre of power—was the keeper of the temporal discipline, fixing time for worshipping practices.[25] Nowadays, we are surrounded by clocks in town and city squares, offices and airports.[26] This proves that the concept of time is intrinsically necessary to the organisation of societies and societal conduct, whereby chronologies and clocks are ways to organise institutions and power.[27]

As it is set to organise societal 'praxis' and 'practices',[28] the concept of 'time' is intrinsically linked to that of 'conduct' in law. Conduct (praxis)[29] that is channelled through norms takes place not only in a specific place but also at a specific time (t) or in time lapses and intervals ($t \rightarrow t$). Thus, for instance, legal outcomes such as the acquisition of property through adverse possession are based on the lapsing of time as required by legal norms.[30] The debate in philosophical, physical and medical sciences tells that time is continuous, requires

21 See F. Bloom, 'The Law's Clock' (2015–2016) 104 *Georgetown Law Journal* 1.

22 J. Barbour, 'The Nature of Time' (2009) ArXiv:0903.3489v1 1, at 3; D. Rooney, *About Time: A History of Civilization in Twelve Clocks*, W.W. Norton and Company, 2021, at 105.

23 E.G. Richards, *Mapping Time: The Calendar and Its History*, Oxford University Press, 1998.

24 Barbour, 'The Nature of Time' (2009) at 3; Rooney, *About Time*, 2021, at 121.

25 D.S. Landes, *Revolution in Time: Clocks and the Making of the Modern World*, Belknap Press of Harvard University Press, 2000, at 48 and 53; K. Birth, *Objects of Time: How Things Shape Temporality*, Palgrave, 2012; McCarthy and Seidelmann, *Time*, 2018, at 148 ff.

26 R. Struthers, *Hands of Time: A Watchmaker's History*, Harper Collins, 2023.

27 Bloom, 'The Law's Clock' (2015–2016) at 9; M. Kreuzer, 'Varieties of Time in Comparative Historical Analysis', in K.H. Goetz (ed.), *The Oxford Handbook of Time and Politics*, Oxford University Press, 2019, 197, at 203.

28 T. Hirsch, *Le temps des sociétés: d'Émile Durkheim à Marc Bloch*, EHESS, 2012.

29 See s. 1.1.

30 C.M. Rose, 'The Law Is Nine-Tenths of Possession: An Adage Turned on Its Head', in Y. Chang (ed.), *Law and Economics of Possession*, Cambridge University Press, 2015, 40, at 53.

change and can be represented as either circular or linear.[31] Linear time can be figured out as an arrow launched from the past, crossing the present and heading to the future (→), tracing a straight line of instants (moments: t_1, t_2, t_3, $t_{4...}$) and expressing the idea of irreversibility ('arrow' of time).[32]

Figure 2.2 Linear time (t→t)

Circular time can be seen as a rotating wheel movement or a rhythmic pendulum oscillation, expressing the idea of cycles and periods repeating over and over again.[33] Linear time is mostly a construct of Western culture and is the standard convention in science, particularly based on the physical theory of the Big Bang.[34] By contrast, circular time is mostly a construct of the Incan, Mayan, Buddhist, Hinduist and Jainist cultures.[35]

Considering that there is no extensive debate on the representation of time in the legal discourse, it can fundamentally be noted that there is no absolute standard to measure time, and it is all a matter of conventions,[36] which entail coordination and the involvement of several organisations, such as the International Earth Rotation and Reference Systems Service, rather than the International Telecommunication Union.[37] The presently dominant European timescale, including a 365-day year (civil time, based on the Roman calendar), a 24-hour day (natural time: an ancient Egyptian formula), a 60-minute hour and a 60-second minute (Babylonian notions), as well as leap years and seconds for consistency with the Earth's rotation and orbit, is the outcome of the sedimentation of cultural knowledge over centuries.[38] On this basis, if we take it as a means of fundamentally organising society temporally, *prima facie*, the structure of the calendar relies on a circular schematisation of time, notably based on recurring years and days.[39] Nonetheless, on closer inspection, as years and days are numbered, ultimately a linear conception of time prevails.[40] Furthermore, change, which provides the basis for a liner conception of time in science, is also a key element determining shifts in

31 C. Callender (ed.), *The Oxford Handbook of Philosophy of Time*, Oxford University Press, 2011.

32 A.S. Eddington, *The Nature of the Physical World*, Cambridge Scholar Publishing, 1927; M. Heidegger, *Sein und Zeit (Being and Time)*, Max Niemeyer Verlag, 1953, tr. J. Stambaugh, State University of New York Press, 1996, at 386; M. Black, 'The "Direction" of Time' (1959) 19(3) *Analysis* 54; H. Price, 'The Flow of Time', in Callender (ed.), *The Oxford Handbook*, 2011, 276.

33 R. Caillois and N. McKeon, 'Circular Time, Rectilinear Time' (1963) 11(42) *Diogenes* 1.

34 J. Barbour, *The End of Time*, Oxford University Press, 2001, at 17–20.

35 B. Adam, *Time*, Polity Press, 2004, at 14–16.

36 H. Poincaré, *The Value of Science*, Science Press, 1907, at 30.

37 McCarthy and Seidelmann, *Time*, 2018, at 316.

38 Levine, 'GPS and the Legal Traceability' (2001) at 53; Birth, 'Standards in the Shadows', 2019, at 199.

39 McCarthy and Seidelmann, *Time*, 2018, at 2.

40 See further Birth, 'Standards in the Shadows', 2019, at 197 ff.

factors underpinning the dimension of time in the law,[41] whereby change is a core factor triggering development in the law.[42] In any case, theoretical legal models should not be considered absolutely exhaustive representations of reality, but rather functional tools that allow predictions on societal events as, eventually, 'all models are wrong, but some are useful'.[43] For the purpose of graph-theoretic notation, on paper, which is a 'static' means, time, which is a 'dynamic' concept based on change, can be conveniently represented chronographically as linear (running in all directions). As a consequence, a 'procedure' can be conceived of as a linear behavioural sequence,[44] which can be particularly visualised through 'verbs as nexus' representation $\left(P_{\rightarrow(no)act(t1)\rightarrow}P_{\rightarrow(no)act(t2)}\right)$.[45] On this basis, a chronographic representation of a procedure can be outlined based on the arrow of time (figure 2.3).

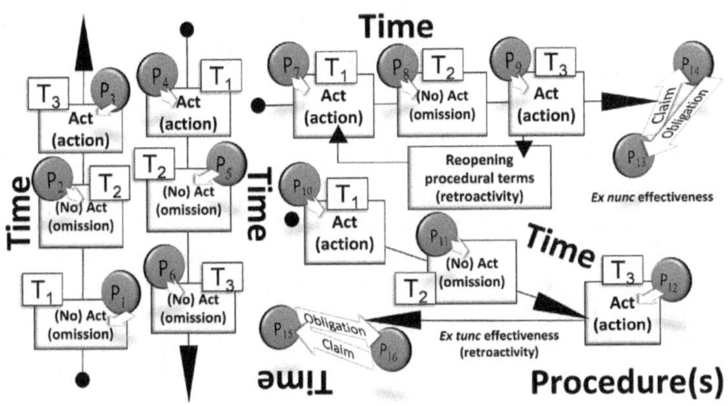

Figure 2.3 Time and procedure(s) $\left(P_{\rightarrow(no)act(t1)\rightarrow}P_{\rightarrow(no)act(t2)}\right)$

In other words, the linear perception of time spawns the concept of a 'procedure' $(P_{\rightarrow(no)act(t1)\rightarrow}P_{\rightarrow(no)act(t2)})$. Within this framework, while the idea of the

41 See, for instance, S. Ranchordás and Y. Roznai (eds.), *Time, Law and Change: An Interdisciplinary Study*, Bloomsbury, 2020; K.P. Van der Ploeg, 'International Law through Time: On Change and Facticity in International Law', in K.P. Van der Ploeg, L. Pasquet and L. Castellanos-Jankiewicz (eds.), *International Law and Time: Narratives and Techniques*, Springer, 2022, 313, at 316.

42 G. Messenger, 'The Development of International Law, Perception and the Problem of Time', in Van der Ploeg, Pasquet and Castellanos-Jankiewicz (eds.), *International Law and Time*, 2022, 335, at 336.

43 G.E.P. Box, 1980.

44 According to Merriam and Webster, a 'procedure' is 'a series of steps followed in a regular definite order' (G. Merriam, C. Merriam and N. Webster, 'Procedure', https://www.merriam-webster.com/dictionary/procedure).

45 Sowa, *Knowledge Representation*, 2000, at 182 and 270 ff.

time arrow running from the past to the present and future leads to a graphic representation through an arrow going from the left to the right (→), other directions cannot be excluded in legal temporality. For instance, procedurally, the discovery of new evidence can lead to a reopening of terms, thus running backwards in time and bringing back the hands of the law clock, which can be conveniently represented through an arrow running (anti-clockwise) from the right to the left (←). Substantively, the law (P—P) can be created, varied or removed retroactively as a result of procedures, whereby norms, claims, obligations, rights and duties apply *ex tunc* (←) rather than *ex nunc* (→),[46] which can also be conveniently represented through an arrow running (anti-clockwise) from the right to the left. Furthermore, administrative procedures involving interaction between agents situated at different hierarchical levels in government entail vertical (↑↓) and horizontal (←→) dynamics.

Within this framework, procedural conduct itself $\left(P_{\rightarrow(\text{no})\text{act}(t1)\rightarrow}P_{\rightarrow(\text{no})\text{act}(t2)}\right)$ is regulated by claim—obligation and right—duty relationships (P—P). For instance, the law of evidence governing judicial proceedings may provide that a party has a right $\left(P_1 - P_{2,3\ldots}\right)$ to examine a witness (t_1)—for example, under section 27 of the Uniform Evidence Act (UEA) in Australia: '[a] party [P_1] may [*right* $P_1 - P_{2,3\ldots}$] question any witness $\left[P_{1\rightarrow\text{ exam }\rightarrow}W\right]$, except as provided by this Act'[47]—which is followed by a right of the opposing party [$P_2 - P_{1,3\ldots}$] to proceed with cross-examination (t_2)—for instance, under UEA section 33: '[u]nless the court otherwise directs . . . cross-examination of a witness $\left[P_{2\rightarrow\text{cr-exam}\rightarrow}W\right]$ is not to take place before [*no-right before* → *right after* $P_2 - P_{1,3\ldots}$] the examination in chief of the witness'[48]—which further entails a right for another party $\left(P_1 - P_{2,3\ldots}\right)$ to proceed with re-examination (t_3)—for instance, under UEA section 28(b): '[u]nless the court otherwise directs . . . re-examination of a witness [$P_{1\rightarrow\text{re-exam}\rightarrow}W$] is not to take place before [*no-right before* → *right after* $P_1 - P_{2,3\ldots}$] all other parties who wish to do so have cross-examined the witness.'[49]

2.3 Linking norms through (vertical and horizontal) procedure(s): normative systems

Legal norms determine the procedures (modalities: P→(no)act(t1)→P→(no)act(t2)) to create, vary, remove and enforce other norms (P—P) within an entirely normative system: every norm is regulated according to the provision of another norm.[50] Given that time represented as a line is at the basis of procedures seen as law-making means $\left(P_{\rightarrow(\text{no})\text{act}(t1)\rightarrow}P_{\rightarrow(\text{no})\text{act}(t2)\rightarrow}P\text{—}P\right)$ and can run

46 Kelsen, *General Theory*, 1945, at 44.
47 Commonwealth of Australia, Uniform Evidence Act, 1995.
48 Commonwealth of Australia, Uniform Evidence Act, 1995.
49 Commonwealth of Australia, Uniform Evidence Act, 1995.
50 Kelsen, *General Theory*, 1945, at 124 and 132.

in all senses on paper, based on a linear—vertical (↑↓) or horizontal (←→)—structure, a procedure may entail both a vertical and horizontal element.

The basic vertical principle to organise norms is hierarchy (↑↓): norms can be interlinked in a superior—subordinate relationship, whereby different regulatory levels exist, according to a static or dynamic paradigm. The static paradigm, which is grounded in natural law, especially as developed by Leibniz, establishes that legal norms are naturally ranked as a *more geometrico demonstrandum* model, whereby rules implicitly develop from one another $\left(P—P\rightarrow P—P\right)$ by reason of their content.[51] By contrast, the dynamic paradigm, which is grounded in legal positivism as particularly developed by Kelsen, establishes that norms are ranked based on their act-sources $\left(P_{\rightarrow(\text{no})\ \text{act}\rightarrow}P—P\right)$, whereby the exercise of power—that is, competence—becomes the key element to shape a legal order as a normative pyramid (↑↓).[52] This approach entails a person who is entrusted by people with the capacity $\left(\text{power: } P_{\text{pow}}\right)$ to require the conduct of another, thus prescribing what to do.[53] Norms are thus created through acts that constitute a dynamic process, whereby the legal system appears as a creative chain $\left(P_{\rightarrow(\text{no})\text{act}(t1)\rightarrow}P_{\rightarrow(\text{no})\text{act}(t2)\rightarrow}P—P\right)$.[54] This approach also fits with the theory of imperatives and performing acts elaborated by Austin, whereby the law is the command of a sovereign authority.[55] Within this framework, public law (claims, obligations, rights and duties) flows from unilateral acts of persons empowered to act so $\left(P_{P\rightarrow(\text{no})\text{act}\rightarrow}P—P\right)$[56] at a macro (economic) level. By contrast, private law (claims, obligations, rights and duties) flows from bilateral or multilateral acts (contractual proposal and acceptance) of persons empowered to act so $\left(P_{\rightarrow(\text{no})\ \text{act}\leftarrow}P_{\rightarrow}P—P\right)$[57] at a micro (economic) level.

51 See von Leibniz, *Nova methodus discendae docendoquae jurisprudentiae*, 1667, Giuffré, 2012, ch. II, at para. 25; C.E. Alchurrón and E. Bulygin, *Normative Systems*, Springer, 1971, at 69; G.W. von Leibniz, 'On Natural Law', in P. Riley (ed.), *Leibniz: Political Writings*, Cambridge University Press, 2nd ed., 1988, 77.

52 Kelsen, *Reine Rechtslehre (Pure Theory)*, 1934, at 195 ff.; Kelsen, *Allgemeine Theorie*, 1979, at 26. See further H. Grotius, *De jure belli ac pacis (On the Law of War and Peace)*, 1625, tr. A.C. Campbell, Createspace, 2017, at 3; Å. Frändberg, *From Rechtsstaat to Universal Law-State: An Essay in Philosophical Jurisprudence*, Springer, 2014, at 56.

53 J.S. Mill, *On Liberty*, 1859, Yale University Press, 2003, at 139; M. Foucault, *Power*, tr. R. Hubley, et al., New York Press, 1994, at 340; S. Bertea, *The Normative Claim of Law*, Hart, 2009, at 17–18; E. Fox-Decent, *Sovereignty's Promise: The State as a Fiduciary*, Oxford University Press, 2011, at 5; A. Halpin, 'Language, Truth and Law', in M. Freeman and F. Smith (eds.), *Law and Language*, Oxford University Press, 2013, 62, at 65.

54 Kelsen, *Reine Rechtslehre (Introduction)*, 1934, at 56; Kelsen, *General Theory*, 1945, at 131–132.

55 Austin, *The Province of Jurisprudence*, 1832, at 24. See further Raz, *Practical Reason*, 1970, at 62; Raz, *The Concept*, 1980, at 6.

56 Kelsen, *Reine Rechtslehre (Pure Theory)*, 1934, at 281; Ross, *Om ret*, 1958, at 202 ff.; Radbruch, *Einführung*, 1980, at 54.

57 Kelsen, *Reine Rechtslehre (Pure Theory)*, 1934, at 281; Ross, *Om ret*, 1958, at 167; Radbruch, *Einführung*, 1980, at 90; E. Bulygin, 'On Norms of Competence', in Bernal, et al. (eds.), *Essays*, 2015, 272, at 273.

The static paradigm, whereby norms are fundamentally elaborated by means of deduction or induction (P—P→P—P), and the dynamic one, where rules proliferate by means of act-sources $\left(P_{\rightarrow(\text{no})\text{act}\rightarrow} P—P\right)$, are not necessarily conflicting with each other; if the act-source remains the fundamental principle vertically organising a legal system, yet other hierarchically ordered norms can statically flow from such set rules $\left(P_{\rightarrow(\text{no})\text{act}\rightarrow}P—P\rightarrow P—P\right)$.[58] This demonstrates that different types of legal reasoning can be developed and sharply coexist with one another to provide a thorough account of the legal order vertically organised as a 'normative pyramid' (↑↓).[59] On this basis, we can outline the following vertical (procedural) pattern:

Law-making (t_1: sources of the law, $P_{P\rightarrow \text{law-making},}P_{\rightarrow \text{law-making}\leftarrow}P$)
→ primary claim—obligation (right—duty) relationship (t_2: P—P)

The vertical structure of a legal system can be represented through Kripke-style semantics.

$$\boldsymbol{Claim}_{p1}(\text{NON})A - \boldsymbol{Obl}_{p2}(\text{NON})A$$
$$\downarrow$$
$$\boldsymbol{Claim}_{p3}(\text{NON})A - \boldsymbol{Obl}_{p4}(\text{NON})A \qquad \boldsymbol{Claim}_{p5}(\text{NON})A - \boldsymbol{Obl}_{p6}(\text{NON})A$$

This matrix can be further translated into graph-theoretic notation (figure 2.4).

The basic horizontal criterion to combine norms is the principle of imputation (causation), which provides that a norm prescribing a duty (1) always entails a secondary norm (2) establishing another duty sanctioning the violation of the primary duty, according to a retributive and coercive process.[60] Actually, this principle expresses the idea that the logical form of a norm is necessarily hypothetical: 'if A is, B ought to be'.[61] Such a formula is a precious attempt to conceive of the law concisely, moving away from natural language and seeking to explain the structural dynamics of normative systems.[62] In this

58 Kelsen, *Reine Rechtslehre (Pure Theory)*, 1934, at 197–198.

59 Kevelson, *The Law as a System*, 1988, at 10.

60 Austin, *The Province of Jurisprudence*, 1832, at 14–15; Ross, *Om ret*, 1958, at 209–210; Raz, *The Concept*, 1970, at 24; R. Nozick, *Philosophical Explanations*, Clarendon Press, 1981, at 363; Nozick, *Socratic Puzzles*, Harvard University Press, 1997, at 15.

61 See Kelsen, *Reine Rechtslehre (Pure Theory)*, 1934, at 89 ff. and 114 ff.; Kelsen, *General Theory*, 1945, at 59. In truth, there are three obligations: A (primary obligation P_1—P_2), B (secondary obligation P_1—P_2), and C 'ought to' (the obligation (of a judge P_p) to impose B (secondary norm: sanction) as a consequence of A (breach of a primary norm)) (see Bobbio, *Essais*, 1998, at 233).

62 On the need to explore and understand the dynamics of normative systems, see Rotolo and Sartor, 'Deductive and Deontic Reasoning', 2018, at 269.

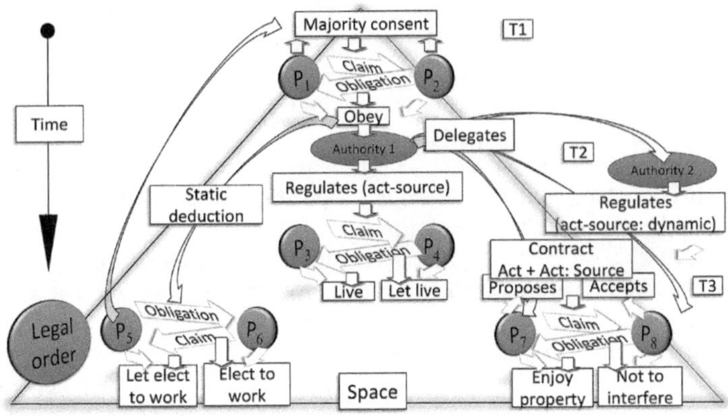

Figure 2.4 (Vertical) Hierarchy $\left(P_{\rightarrow \text{law-making} \rightarrow} P—P \rightarrow P—P\right)$

scheme, 'A' is the violation of a claim—obligation or right—duty relationship and expresses nothing other than the idea of 'unlawful conduct', that is, the conduct of a person contrary to—not right: breaching $\left(P_{\rightarrow \text{breach}}\right)$—an obligation—claim or duty—right relationship (1). By contrast, 'B' is the obligation—claim or duty—right relationship (2) sanctioning the violation.[63] This expresses the concept of 'responsibility' and the procedural idea that the violation of an obligation or a duty (norm 1: P—P) triggers the application of another obligation or duty as a sanction (norm 2: P—P).[64] Through the lens of basic deontic modalities, such a conditional conception of the legal norm simply means that the violation of a duty entails the application of a duty as a sanction $\left((1)P—P_{\rightarrow \text{breach} \rightarrow} P—P(2)\right)$. Arguably, only because of the transgression of a rule can one become better aware of the existence of a logically prior norm.[65] Indeed, a lot has been written on the question as to whether claims, obligations, rights and duties can be considered effective if they are not complemented by enforcing sanctions, whereby the effectiveness (validity) of a primary norm (1) becomes fundamentally dependent on the application of a (sanctioning) secondary norm (2), ultimately conceiving of an 'obligation'

63 See Drago, 'La notion d'obligation' (2000) at 43–44.

64 Kelsen, *General Theory*, 1945, at 59–60 and 65.

65 Heraclitus, *Fragments*, Penguin Putnam, 2003, fr. 23: 'Men would not have known the name of justice [from Latin '*ius*', '*iustum*', i.e. '*rectum*', 'straight', 'right'] if these things [instances of injustice] had not occurred'. See further M. Foucault, *Surveiller et punir*, Gallimard, 1975.

and a 'duty' as the 'fear of a sanction'.[66] In essence, it is undeniable that a person has a legal obligation to follow a certain course of conduct to the extent that opposite conduct is established in a legal norm as the condition for the application of a sanction and ensuing coercive action as a consequence of unlawful conduct.[67]

The principle of imputation is a procedural concept and, thus, a dynamic one. It is implemented and, therefore, spelled out in detail through adjudication procedures. In fact, the infringement of a primary obligation or duty (1: P—P) by a person $\left(P_{\rightarrow \text{breach}}\right)$ triggers different procedures, notably mediation, conciliation, arbitration and judicial proceedings, which aim at assessing the violation and applying—or not applying, varying and removing—a secondary obligation or duty as a sanction (2: P—P). Along these lines, Ross goes to the extent of considering that a claim is just the necessary condition for suit and judgment against a person.[68] Within such procedures, organs—particularly mediators, conciliators, arbitrators and judges—are empowered to apply $\left(P_{P\rightarrow \text{decision}}\right)$ sanctions (2) as a legal consequence of the breach of a primary obligation (1).[69] It is therefore clear that adjudication organs and procedures have a law-making function, which entails the creation of legal norms $\left(P_{P\rightarrow \text{adj}(t1)\rightarrow}P_{\rightarrow \text{adj}(t2)\rightarrow}P\text{—}P\right)$.[70]

To ensure the effective implementation of a sanction, guaranteeing the efficacy of the principle of imputation, enforcement procedures are deployed when a person (P) who is the addressee of a sanctioning obligation (P—P) infringes it $\left(P_{\rightarrow \text{breach}}\right)$.[71] Indeed, without adequate enforcement procedures, a sanction would not be effective as its retributive nature would be lost. Thus, it is considered that the effectiveness of primary obligations (1) is eventually proportionate to the frequency of application of sanctions (2) and their enforcement.[72] While they are not primarily law-making mechanisms, to the extent that they do not necessarily—but can (accessorily)—create, vary or remove claims, obligations, rights and duties (P—P), enforcement procedures are essential to the functioning of the law as a normative system, insofar as they implement secondary obligations (P—P) and guarantee the efficacy of

66 Kelsen, *General Theory*, 1945, 59 and 72. Critically, see Ross, *Om ret*, 1958, at 52.

67 Kelsen, *Reine Rechtslehre (Introduction)*, 1934, at 43; Hart, *The Concept*, 1961, at 93; J. Raz, *The Authority of Law*, Oxford University Press, 2nd ed., 2009, at 236.

68 Ross, *Om ret*, 1958, at 163.

69 Llewellyn, *The Theory*, 2011, at 37 and 67.

70 Kelsen, *General Theory*, 1945 at 134; R. Dworkin, *Law's Empire*, Hart, 1998, 3–6; E.W. Thomas, *The Judicial Process: Realism, Pragmatism, Reasoning and Principles*, Cambridge University Press, 2005, at 3.

71 Ross, *Om ret*, 1958, at 206 and 210–211.

72 Perrin, *Pour une théorie de la connaissance*, 1979, at 92–93.

legal norms.[73] This leads to outlining the following horizontal (procedural) pattern:

Primary obligation—claim (duty—right) relationship (t_1: P—P (1))
→ infringement (t_2: liability $P_{\rightarrow breach}$)
→ dispute settlement procedure (t_3: $P_{P\rightarrow settlement}$, $P_{\rightarrow settlement\leftarrow}P$)
→ secondary obligation—claim (duty—right) relationship (t_4: sanction P—P (2))
→ infringement (t_5: liability $P_{\rightarrow breach}$)
→ enforcement (t_6: $P_{P\rightarrow enforcement}$, $P_{\leftarrow enforcement\leftarrow}P$)

The principle of imputation can be represented through Kripke-style semantics.

$$\boldsymbol{Obl}_{p1}(\text{NON})\text{A} - \boldsymbol{Claim}_{p2}(\text{NON})\text{A} \rightarrow \boldsymbol{Obl}_{p1}(\text{NON})\text{A} - \boldsymbol{Claim}_{p2}(\text{NON})\text{A}$$

The matrix can be translated into graph-theoretic notation (figure 2.5).

Such procedures can be declined according to various modalities. For instance, under administrative procedures, if a public agent St_{P1} breaches $(St_{P1\rightarrow breach})$ the obligation not to act in excess of power vis-à-vis P_2 $(St_{P1} - P_2)$ and imposes expropriation, P_2 will be empowered to enter a recourse with an administrative tribunal $(P_{2\rightarrow rec\rightarrow}St_P)$, instructing a procedure to gather evidence and deliver a decision imposing a sanction $(St_{P\rightarrow sanct})$, for example, a mandamus and certiorari to reprocess expropriation. If St_{P1} further does not comply with the sanction $(St_{P1\rightarrow breach})$, P_2 will be empowered to enter another recourse with administrative tribunals $(P_{2\rightarrow rec\rightarrow}St_P)$, which will nominate an *ad hoc* public commissioner reprocessing the decision invalidated $(St_{P\rightarrow nom\rightarrow}St_{P\rightarrow repr})$.[74] In

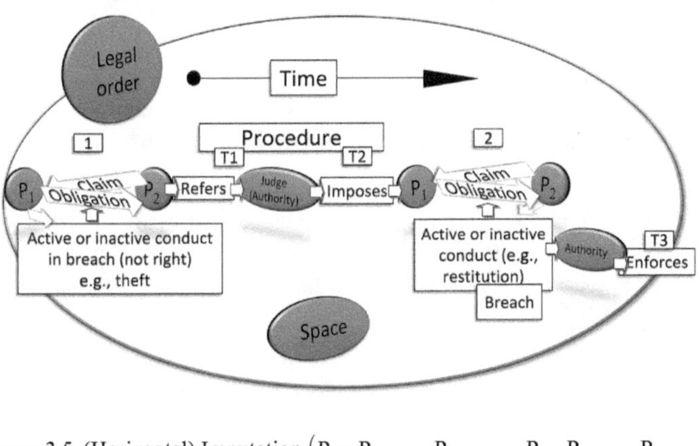

Figure 2.5 (Horizontal) Imputation $(P—P_{\rightarrow breach\rightarrow}P_{\rightarrow settlement\rightarrow}P—P_{\rightarrow breach\rightarrow}P_{\rightarrow enforcement})$

73 See W. Read, *Legal Thinking: Its Limits and Tensions*, University of Pennsylvania Press, 1986, at 164.

74 See, for instance, P. Leyland and G. Anthony, *Administrative Law*, Oxford University Press, 8th ed., 2016, at 441 ff.

tort proceedings, if P_1 breaches $(P_{1\rightarrow breach})$ the claim to payment vis-à-vis $P_2(P_1 - P_2)$ by not fulfilling a contractual debt, P_2 will have the power to complain with a judge $(P_{2\rightarrow rec\rightarrow}St_P)$, entering proceedings leading to a sanctioning injunction $(St_{P\rightarrow sanct})$ imposing performance of the contractual obligation $(P_{1\rightarrow perf})$. In the case of further non-compliance $(P_{1\rightarrow breach})$, a public officer will proceed to enforcement by seizing property and compensating $P_2(St_{P\rightarrow enf})$.[75] In criminal proceedings, if P_1 breaches P_2's right to property $(P_1 - P_{2,3...})$ by committing theft $(P_{1\rightarrow breach})$, any person (P) will be enabled to complain with a public prosecutor $(P_{\rightarrow rec\rightarrow}St_P)$, whereby a judicial procedure will ensue to collect evidence and deliver a decision imposing a sanction $(St_{P\rightarrow sanct})$, for instance, imprisonment. If P_1 further does not comply with the sanction $(P_{1\rightarrow breach})$, the enforcement authority—notably, a state officer—will enforce the sanction $(St_{P\rightarrow enf})$ by incarcerating P_1.[76]

The coexistence of essential vertical and horizontal (procedural) criteria interconnecting legal norms confirms that different types of legal reasoning can not only sharply coexist with one another[77] but are also indispensable to a coherent and thorough understanding of the mechanics of the legal system. We therefore have the following pattern (procedure):

Law-making procedure (t_1: $P_{P\rightarrow law\text{-}making,}P_{\rightarrow law\text{-}making\leftarrow}P$)
→ primary obligation—claim (duty—right) relationship (t_2: P—P (1))
→ infringement (t_3: liability $P_{\rightarrow breach}$)
→ dispute settlement procedure (t_4: $P_{P\rightarrow settlement,}P_{\rightarrow settlement\leftarrow}P$))
→ secondary obligation—claim (duty—right) relationship (t_5: sanction P—P (2))
→ infringement (t_6: liability $P_{\rightarrow breach}$)
→ enforcement (t_7: $P_{P\rightarrow enforcement,}P_{\leftarrow enforcement\leftarrow}P$)

2.4 Substantive and procedural norms: a consistent normative scheme (substance as procedure and procedure as substance)

Based on their combining criteria, norms can be distinguished from one another and ranged into different taxonomies. The most fundamental classification relies on the distinction between 'primary' (1) and 'secondary' (2)

75 See, for example, N.J. McBride and R. Bagshaw, *Tort Law*, Pearson, 6th ed., 2018, at 797 ff.
76 See, for instance, W.P. Signorelli, *Criminal Law, Procedure and Evidence*, Routledge, 2nd ed., 2024.
77 Rawls, *A Theory*, 1971, at 47–48; Kevelson, *The Law as a System*, 1988 at 10.

norms, which can assume different meanings,[78] particularly following the principles of (horizontal (→)) imputation and (vertical (↑↓)) hierarchy.

According to Kelsen and most scholars, based on the horizontal (→) principle of imputation, primary norms simply regulate claims, obligations, rights and duties (1: P—P), whereas secondary norms regulate claims, obligations, rights and duties imposed as sanctions (2: P—P) following the breach of primary rules $\left((1)\ \text{P—P}_{\rightarrow \text{breach} \rightarrow}\text{P—P}\ (2)\right)$.[79] Since the principle of imputation expresses nothing other than the hypothetical logical form of a norm, it is possible to subsume primary norms into the category of secondary rules: an obligation cannot be conceived of without a sanction for its violation, so establishing a unique category of norms (P—P: 1). These are 'substantive' rules—that is, norms that regulate the conduct of persons acting in society (substance: $\text{P—P}_{\rightarrow \text{(no)act}}$)—which are considered to be given per se and are also known as 'self-regarding rights' or 'telic rules'.[80]

On this basis, according to Hart, in light of the vertical (↑↓) hierarchical paradigm, primary norms—that is, substantive rules—regulate obligations and sanctions (1: P—P), whereas secondary norms regulate the ability to act on primary norms by exerting legal competency $\left(2\text{: } \text{P}_{\text{P}\rightarrow \text{(no)act,}}\text{P}_{\rightarrow \text{(no)act}\leftarrow}\text{P})\right)$—that is, regulatory power—to create, vary, remove and enforce substantive claims, obligations, rights and duties (P—P).[81] Such a less common interpretation is useful to define the concept of 'power' in a normative sense and fundamentally identifies secondary norms (2) with procedural rules—that is, norms that regulate the procedure (or procedures) which are defined as 'adjective law'[82] or 'law of action' $\left(\text{P}_{\text{P}\rightarrow \text{(no)act,}}\text{P}_{\rightarrow \text{(no)act}\leftarrow}\text{P}\right)$[83] and are popularly known as 'bureaucracy'—as complementary to primary substantive claims, obligations, rights and duties (P—P). Because of their complementary nature, procedural norms are also known as 'instrumental rules'.[84]

Different normative taxonomies can be useful to clarify legal logic. However, aiming to keep the analysis as simple as possible, we note that the fundamental elementary normative concepts of a 'person' (P), 'legal relationship' (P—P) and 'conduct' $\left(\text{A or NON-A: } \text{P}_{\rightarrow \text{(no)act}}\right)$ inhere consistently in all legal norms and define their constant formal scheme. The taxonomic criteria, which can be multiplied indefinitely, can always be brought back to such three necessary conditions. Thus, whereas in Hart's view the concept of 'power' is the

78 Bobbio, *Essais*, 1998, at 159 ff.

79 Kelsen, *Allgemeine Theorie*, 1979, at 142.

80 See J. Bentham, *Works*, Bowring's ed., 1843, at 5–6; A. Kocourek, *An Introduction to the Science of Law*, Cambridge University Press, 1930, at 312; Kocourek, 'Substance and Procedure' (1941) 10 *Fordham Law Review* 157, at 164.

81 See Hart, *The Concept*, 1961, at 94.

82 T.E. Holland, *The Elements of Jurisprudence*, MacMillan, 1880, at 238.

83 J. Salmond, *Jurisprudence*, Sweet & Maxwell, 6th ed., 1924, at 495, para. 172.

84 Kocourek, *An Introduction*, 1930, at 307; Kocourek, 'Substance and Procedure' (1941) at 164.

basic principle underpinning secondary norms, it can be more simply embedded, along the lines of the theory developed by Kelsen, in that of a 'faculty', which can be regarded as 'a right to act upon rights' $\left(P\text{—}P_{\rightarrow(\text{no})\text{act}\rightarrow}P\text{—}P\right)$.[85] Indeed, a 'subjective right' can be seen as a competence to participate in creating the law and as a 'particular shaping of the law-creating function', that is, as 'a possible way of shaping the content of the objective law' $\left(P_{\text{right}\rightarrow\text{law-making}}\right)$.[86] In fact, procedural norms are also known as 'other-regarding rights' and it is common in the legal context to speak of a 'right to legislative initiative', a 'right to give evidence' and a 'right to appeal'.[87] In a simple model, the expression 'adjective law' captures the idea of procedural rules as ancillary claims, obligations, rights and duties (P—P: 2) aiming to create, vary, remove and enforce 'substantive law' as a set of claims, obligations, rights and duties (P—P: 1) governing societal conduct. From an alternative but complementary perspective, 'power' can also be regarded as a subjective quality (a positional structure: P_{pow})—that is, an institutional quality of the person in office—empowering a person to 'act' and create, vary, remove or enforce claims, obligations, rights and duties[88]—that is, producing legal effects (P—P)[89]—within the limits defined by legal obligations and duties (P—P).[90] Such a perspective does not multiply objective legal notions because it predicates the right to act upon rights as an attribute of a person, whereby a legal subject is 'empowered' to act and regulate legal relationships $\left(P_{\text{pow}\rightarrow(\text{no})\text{act}\rightarrow}P\text{—}P\right)$.

In light of the hypothetical scheme according to which 'if A is, B ought to be', given that procedural conduct $\left(\text{action or inaction: } P_{P\rightarrow(\text{no})\text{act}}, P_{\rightarrow(\text{no})\text{act}\leftarrow}P\right)$ eventually aims at regulating claim—obligation (or obligation—claim) and right—duty (or duty—right) relationships (P—P), it is possible to conceive of a legal order—that is, the law—simply as a procedural system, whereby there is no difference between substantive and procedural law as both are concerned with claim—obligation (or obligation—claim) and right—duty (or duty—right) relationships (P—P) that regulate conduct (action or inaction) among persons in defined space and time $\left(P\text{—}P_{\rightarrow(\text{no})\text{act}(\text{sp/t})}\right)$. This approach tends to rejoin the Austinian stance, which denies the distinction between 'substantive'

85 Frändberg, *From Rechtsstaat to Universal Law-State*, 2014, at 174.

86 Kelsen, *Reine Rechtslehre (Introduction)*, 1934, at 44, 45 and 46.

87 See s. 2.2 and s. 3.4.

88 See J. Austin, *Lectures on Jurisprudence: The Philosophy of Positive Law*, J. Murray, 4th ed., 1875, at 359; Kelsen, *Allgemeine Theorie*, 1945, at 102; Raz, *Practical Reason*, 1970, at 98; R. Lukic, *Théorie de l'Etat et du droit*, Dalloz, 1974, at 422; Perrin, *Pour une théorie de la connaissance*, 1979, at 43; Sartor, *Legal Reasoning*, 2007, at 577 ff.; G. Sartor, 'Fundamental Legal Concepts: A Formal and Teleological Characterisation' (2006) 14 *AI & Law* (2006) 101, at 120 ff.; M. La Torre, *Law as Institution*, Springer, 2010, at 159.

89 Ross, *Om ret*, 1958, at 166.

90 C. Perelman, *Études de logique juridique*, Bruylant, 1978, Vol. VII, at 15; Read, *Legal Thinking*, 1986, at 75–76.

and 'procedural' rules.[91] Along these lines, some scholars regard the law as 'a process of continuous change', involving 'processes of normative claims and responses to such claims'.[92] This applies not only to Hart's 'primary' norms—that is, substantive norms on rights and duties $\left(P_{\rightarrow(\text{no})\text{act}—\text{act}(\text{no})\leftarrow}P\right)$—but also to Hart's 'secondary' norms—that is, norms of production (procedural norms: $P—P_{\text{pow}\rightarrow(\text{no})\text{act}(t1)\rightarrow}P—P_{\text{pow}\rightarrow(\text{no})\text{act}(t2)}$). Indeed, the notion of a 'right' has been defined particularly as an expression of will, notably through a complaint $\left(P_{\rightarrow\text{compl}}\right)$ that addresses the consequences of unlawful conduct $\left(P_{\rightarrow\text{breach}}\right)$.[93]

Although a simplified approach to legal thinking is probably less elegant than that developed by Hart, it is conceptually more streamlined and therefore simpler. It confirms that the structure of a norm is universal and permanent (P—P) as fundamentally pointed out by Kelsen.[94] It permits achieving a uniform representation and formalisation of the law, whereby both primary and secondary Hart's norms—that is, all norms—can be visualised according to network theory through simplified graph-theoretic notation.

2.5 Legal persons as normative systems and formal deontic networks

Persons—or subjects—can be simple or complex. Natural persons are simple subjects (P) of claims, obligations, rights and duties. Legal persons (entities) are complex subjects, which are nothing other than legal orders, to the extent that they aggregate physical (and possibly legal) persons—that is, simple and complex subjects—(3) who are linked by claim—obligation and right—duty relationships (1: P—P), which regulate conduct $\left(\text{action or inaction: } P_{\rightarrow(\text{no})\,\text{act}}\right)$ (2) in defined space (sp: 4) and time (t: 5).

Legal persons (entities) are therefore deontic networks (P—P—P). In other words, in order to define legal entities, it is sufficient to consider legal orders by focusing primarily on their subjective elements and secondarily on their (internal) objective relationships. This view fits with the idea that the legal system includes a network of competing legal subsystems, which would be nothing other than legal persons and are thus complex systems of signs and sign relationships referring to social institutions.[95] It also accounts for the assumption that legal codes function as symbolic signs and are mirrors for societal dynamics, whereby the chain of social relationships and judicial

91 Austin, *Lectures on Jurisprudence*, 1875, at 374. See further W.W. Cook, '"Substance" and "Procedure" in the Conflict of Laws' (1933) 42 *Yale Law Journal* 333, at 337.

92 Van der Ploeg, 'International Law through Time' (2022) at 316 and 319.

93 Kelsen, *Reine Rechtslehre (Introduction)*, 1934, at 44.

94 Kelsen, *Reine Rechtslehre (Introduction)*, 1934, at 10 and 26.

95 Kevelson, *The Law as a System*, 1988, at 10–11.

decisions are seen as signs of argument structure.[96] A 'legal person' is therefore the 'personification of a norm complex' as part of the comprehensive system of 'objective law' whereby the claim of one is always matched by the obligation of another, and the right of one is always matched by the duty of others.[97]

Seeing legal persons as normative systems (P—P—P) reconciles the normative conception of the law, particularly as formulated by Kelsen, with the institutional approach, subsuming the institutional aspect, which is predominant in the theory of Romano,[98] into the norm. Indeed, the institutional theory assumes that a legal system includes different parts and, in addition to legal norms, encompasses institutions as complex and diverse separate entities, particularly organised for creating and enforcing legal rules. Within this framework, legal norms would be the ultimate aim of legal institutions, whereby a clear distinction emerges between legal persons—as subjects of norms—and legal norms, prioritising the former over the latter. However, the institutional perspective is more complex than the normative view, which therefore simplifies legal reasoning: it is possible to conceive of persons as normative systems, whereby, of course, norms have a specific content, aiming to define an institutional structure based on claims, obligations, rights and duties.

In other words, legal systems can be seen as persons linked by norms regulating claim—obligation and right—duty relationships (institutional theory) or, the other way around, as norms regulating claim—obligation (or obligation—claim) and right—duty (or duty—right) relationships among persons (normative theory). In the normative theory, legal persons are understood as constructs that exist purely in the legal realm, whereby the law creates normative entities rather than providing pre-existing entities with legal status.[99] Quite effectively, a 'legal person' has been defined as the 'unity of a complex of norms, that is, as a 'legal system governing the behaviour of a plurality of human beings'.[100] In this context, a legal person—or subject—becomes the 'personification' of a 'comprehensive legal system' or of a 'subsystem', that is, a 'subcommunity', grounded in the association's founding instrument.[101] Thus, a legal person is simply a normative taxonomy—that is, a legal scheme—classifying human conduct according to claims, obligations, rights and duties

96 Kevelson, *The Law as a System*, 1988, at 11 and G. Dietze, 'The Limited Rationality of Law', in C.G. Friedrich (ed.), *Rational Decision*, Transaction Publisher, 1964, 63.

97 Kelsen, *Reine Rechtslehre (Introduction)*, 1934, at 51.

98 See S. Romano, *L'ordinamento giuridico (The Legal Order)*, 1917, tr. M. Croce, Routledge, 2017, at 6–7. See also J. Dabin, *Théorie générale du droit*, Dalloz, 1969, at 99; La Torre, *Law as Institution*, 2010, at 97 ff.

99 V.A.J. Kurki, *Legal Personhood*, Cambridge University Press, 2023, at 20 ff.

100 Kelsen, *Reine Rechtslehre (Introduction)*, 1934, at 48.

101 Kelsen, *Reine Rechtslehre (Introduction)*, 1934, at 48.

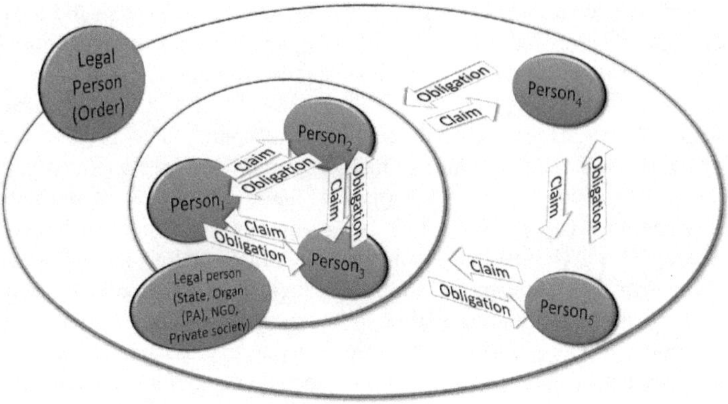

Figure 2.6 Legal person (deontic network) (P—P—P)

(P—P—P).[102] The idea of a legal person as a normative system—that is, as a deontic network—can be simply visualised through graph-theoretic notation (figure 2.6).

Along these lines, scholars have underscored the centrality of the concept of 'legal personality' as a doctrinal category that 'holds together bundles of rights and obligations',[103] whereby legal personhood is defined as a 'cluster property', comprising a single cluster or multiple clusters of legal relationships, depending on their nature and purpose, creating thick and large (P═P═P═P) or thin and small (P—P—P) bundles, depending on different legal persons in variable legal contexts.[104] Legal personhood thus appears as a cluster of severable claims, obligations, rights and duties—that is, as a normative cluster—and emerges as a conceptual scheme whereby norms aggregate to define a 'unit' or 'node' (•), contributing to categorising norms. More specifically, according to bundle theory, legal personhood involves the endowment of a person with claims, rights and further competences $\left(\text{P—P}_{\text{Pcomp}}\right)$.[105] By means of such competences $\left(\text{P}_{\text{Ppow}}\right)$, a legal person can outline $\left(\text{P}_{\text{Ppow}\rightarrow\text{(no)act}}\right)$ normative claims, obligations, rights and duties (P—P) and determine its (internal) individual components. Bundle theory thus expresses the idea that human beings have a network of claims, obligations, rights and duties collectively ((P—P)═P), according to the rules of the legal person as a legal subsystem, which acts as a 'unity', that is, a centre of 'imputation' (node: (•))

102 Kurki, *Legal Personhood*, 2023, at 23.

103 C. Novelli, G. Bongiovanni and G. Sartor, 'A Conceptual Framework for Legal Personality and Its Application to AI' (2022) 13(2) *Jurisprudence* 194.

104 N. Naffine, *Law's Meaning of Life: Philosophy, Religion, Darwin and the Legal Person*, Hart Publishing, 2009, at 46.

105 Kurki, *A Theory*, 2019, at 5.

for normative relationships (ties: —).[106] This approach fits with the idea of seeing legal relationships as fluid 'normative flows' that are created by multiple centres of power and surround persons, rather than conceiving of them as a static paradigm.[107]

As legal persons are artificial constructs that span NGOs, private corporations and public administrations, including municipalities and States,[108] it is possible to conceive of a State (that is, the core node (•) of the law or the 'comprehensive legal system'[109]) as an aggregation of persons linked by norms regulating claim—obligation (or obligation—claim) and right—duty (or duty—right) relationships (institutional theory) or the other way around, as a set of norms regulating claim—obligation (or obligation—claim) and right—duty (or duty—right) relationships among persons (normative theory). From a normative perspective, the State appears as a system of claims, obligations, rights and duties, and seeing the State as a normative system further leads to the possibility of visualising it as a deontic network (P=P=P). Internally, the State encompasses further physical (P) and legal (P—P—P) persons, to which it delegates competences to create, vary and remove normative legal relationships $\left(St_{Ppow \rightarrow (no)act \rightarrow} P\text{—}P\right)$.[110] Externally, the State can aggregate with other States—and possibly with other legal persons—to constitute international organisations, which are legal persons, that is, deontic networks, endowed with sovereign power (IO: St—St).[111]

106 Kelsen, *Reine Rechtslehre (Introduction)*, 1934, at 50.
107 E. Nicolas, *Penser les flux normatifs: essai sur le droit fluide*, Mare & Martin, 2018, at 24–28.
108 Kurki, *A Theory*, 2019, at 7.
109 Kelsen, *Reine Rechtslehre (Introduction)*, 1934, at 48.
110 Kelsen, *Reine Rechtslehre (Introduction)*, 1934, at 49.
111 H. Kelsen, *Principles of International Law*, Rinehart & Company, 1952, at 178 ff.

3 The State, international law and EU law as normative systems

Formal deontic networks

3.1 States as legal persons, normative systems and formal deontic networks

Since the peace of Westphalia in 1648, in terms of personality, the State has become the fundamental unit of the legal system or, we could say, of all legal systems, so much so that we speak of '*Rechtsstaat*' as the 'rule of law'.[1] Indeed, the State is the fundamental unit of geopolitical division around the globe.[2] As a legal person, under article 1 of the 1933 Montevideo Convention on the Rights and Duties of States (CRDS),[3] a State includes three elements: a permanent population (people: St_{peop}), a defined territory (St_{sp}) and a government (St_{Gov}), which further trigger capacity to enter into relations with other States (St—St). This is the inheritance of the historical development of the law based on the concept of a nation-state established since the peace of Westphalia.[4] Subjectively, a State can therefore be defined as an aggregation of people—including both natural and legal persons and defining the personal sphere of validity of the State as a legal order—ruled by a government regulating $\left(St_{Gov\rightarrow reg}\right)$ claim—obligation (or obligation—claim) and right—duty (or duty—right) relationships (P—P) within a defined three-dimensional territory.[5] Objectively, a State can be defined as a system of norms regulating claim—obligation (or obligation—claim) and right—duty (or duty—right)

1 G. Radbruch, *Rechts-Philosophie*, K.F. Koehler Verlag, 1975, at 280; Frändberg, *From Rechtsstaat to Universal Law-State*, 2014, at 23. Critically, see M. Van Hoecke, 'Do "Legal Systems" Exist? The Concept of Law and Comparative Law', in S.P. Donlan and L.H. Urscheler (eds.), *Concepts of Law: Comparative, Jurisprudential, and Social Science Perspectives*, Ashgate, 2014, 43, at 52 ff.

2 P. Bourdieu, *Sur l'État*, Seuil, 2012, at 4; P. Schiff Berman, *Global Legal Pluralism*, Cambridge University Press, 2012, at 62–63.

3 Opened for signature 26 December 1933, 165 League of Nations Treaty Series 19, entered into force 26 December 1934.

4 J.E. Nijman, *The Concept of International Legal Personality: An Inquiry into the History and Theory of International Law*, TMC Asser Press, 2004.

5 See Kelsen, *General Theory*, 1945, at 233.

DOI: 10.4324/9781003228318-4

relationships (P—P (1)), and thus conduct $\left(P_{\rightarrow(\text{no})\text{act}}(2)\right)$, between people—including both natural and legal persons (P=P=P (3))—within a defined territory (space (4)) and time (t (5)):[6] $P_{1,2\ldots\text{claim(right)}\rightarrow(\text{no})\text{act}—\text{act(no)}\leftarrow(\text{duty})\text{obl}\ldots 4,3}P$.

The specificity of the State as a legal person (the reason for being the fundamental unit of the legal order) is the fact that it exercises sovereign power $\left(St_{\text{sov}}\right)$,[7] meaning it can create, vary, remove and enforce claim—obligation and right—duty relationships (P—P) unilaterally $\left(t_1\text{: } St_{\text{Gov}\rightarrow(\text{no})\text{act}\rightarrow}P—P\right)$ within its territory.[8] Indeed, sovereignty is supreme and recognises no superior authority (*superiorem non recognoscens*), so much so that States are equally sovereign (*par in parem non habet imperium*: $St_{\text{sov}=\text{sov}}St$),[9] as clarified in CRDS article 4. The State is thus 'government': that is, the 'authority', including a system of public organs and agents $\left(St_{P-P}\right)$ exerting sovereign power (*imperium*) over people.[10] Contrary to the State, natural persons, NGOs and corporations within a State cannot act unilaterally but can only act bilaterally or multilaterally as private subjects via contractual power $\left(t_1\text{: } P_{1\rightarrow(\text{no})\text{act}\leftarrow}P_2\right)$ to create, vary and remove claims, obligations, rights and duties (P—P).

The notion of a state 'territory' (space (•)) is three-dimensional,[11] given that it encompasses ground, atmospheric space above the ground (up to around 62 miles above sea level),[12] exploitable underground and the territorial sea, that is, waters extending as far as 12 nautical miles from the baseline of a coastal State, as established in articles 2 and 3 of the UN Convention on the Law of the Sea (UNCLOS).[13] Moreover, a State has specific rights within the contiguous zone (UNCLOS article 33), extending up to 24 nautical miles from the coast baseline, and the exclusive economic zone (EEZ), covering a maximum of 200 nautical miles from the outer limit of territorial waters (UNCLOS articles 55–57). A State also enjoys specific rights on the continental shelf, which underlies the EEZ and can be extended further to a maximum of 350 nautical miles (UNCLOS article 76). By contrast, the high seas, the

6 Kelsen, *General Theory*, 1945, at 182.

7 'Sovereignty' is indeed the legal translation of the political concept of 'power' underpinned by interest (see H.J. Morgenthau, *Politics among Nations: The Struggle for Power and Peace*, Knopf, 1948).

8 See also Hart, *The Concept*, 1961, at 220; H. Kelsen, *The Communist Theory of Law*, Scientia Verlag Aalen, 1976, at 148; S. Humphreys, *Theatre of the Rule of Law: Transnational Legal Intervention in Theory and Practice*, Cambridge University Press, 2010, 98; Llewellyn, *The Theory*, 2011, at 63 and 67.

9 N. Roughan, *Authorities: Conflicts, Cooperation, and Transnational Legal Theory*, Oxford University Press, 2013, at 178.

10 Kelsen, *Reine Rechtslehre (Pure Theory)*, 1934, at 290.

11 Kelsen, *General Theory*, 1945, at 217.

12 Committee on the Peaceful Uses of Outer Space (COPUOS), Definition and Delimitation of Outer Space, UN Doc. A/AC.105/C.2/2022/CRP.24, 6 April 2022.

13 Opened for signature 10 December 1982, 1833 UN Treaty Series 396, entered into force 16 November 1994.

international seabed area, Antarctica—which is subject to frozen sovereign claims under article 4(2) of the Antarctic Treaty[14]—and outer space beyond approximately 62 miles above sea level are *res communes omnium*: that is, common spaces owned by no one and subject to use by all (UNCLOS article 87; Antarctic Treaty article 4(2); Outer Space Treaty article 4).[15] Furthermore, ships are considered to be under the jurisdiction of the State whose flag they fly and are indeed regarded as an extension of the 'territory' of that State (Geneva Convention on the High Seas article 5;[16] UNCLOS article 91).[17] Similar principles apply to aircraft under article 6 of the 1919 Convention Relating to the Regulation of Aerial Navigation,[18] as well as articles 17 and 19 of the Convention on International Civil Aviation.[19] Under article 8 of the 1967 Outer Space Treaty, a State of registration has 'jurisdiction and control' over objects in outer space.

The dichotomy between 'public' and 'private' persons is mirrored in the international sphere. Indeed, internationally, individuals, NGOs and corporations can only act through contracts $\left(t_1\text{: } P_{\rightarrow \text{contract} \leftarrow} P\right)$ under 'private' international law, for instance, to regulate an extra-territorial sale of products (P—P), and under the Vienna Convention on Contracts for the International Sale of Goods (VCCISG).[20] By contrast, States exercise sovereign power and can thus create, vary and remove interstate legal relationships (St—St) under 'public' international law, notably by means of treaties and customary practices $\left(t_1\text{: } St_{\rightarrow \text{treaty/custom} \leftarrow} St\right)$, as codified in article 38 of the Statute of the International Court of Justice (ICJ).[21] They can also privately regulate

14 Opened for signature 1 December 1959, 402 UN Treaty Series 71, entered into force 23 June 1961.

15 Treaty on Principles Governing the Activities of States in the Exploration and Use of Outer Space, Including the Moon and Other Celestial Bodies, opened for signature 27 January 1967, 610 UN Treaty Series 205, entered into force 10 October 1967.

16 Opened for signature 29 April 1958, 450 UN Treaty Series 82, entered into force 30 September 1962.

17 *M/V 'Saiga' (Saint Vincent and the Grenadines v. Guinea) (No. 2)*, International Tribunal for the Law of the Sea (ITLOS), Judgment of 1 July 1999 (1999) ITLOS Reports 10, at 42, para. 83.

18 Opened for signature 13 October 1919, no longer in force.

19 Opened for signature 7 December 1944, 15 UN Treaty Series 295, entered into force 4 April 1947.

20 Opened for signature 11 April 1980, 1489 UN Treaty Series 3, entered into force 1 January 1988. See further H. Muir Watt (ed.), *Private International Law and Public Law*, Edward Elgar 2015, Vol. I, at 5 ff.; Muir Watt, vol. II, at 5 ff.; M. Belegu, 'Convention for International Sale of Goods in the Internal Law' (2021) 10(special) *Perspectives of Law and Public Administration* 113.

21 Opened for signature 26 June 1945, 1 UN Treaty Series XVI, entered into force 24 October 1945. See further R. Kwiecień, 'The Formal Sources of International Law, the Relationship between Treaties and Custom, and the International Law-Making Process' (2022) 40(1) *Australian Yearbook of International Law* 46.

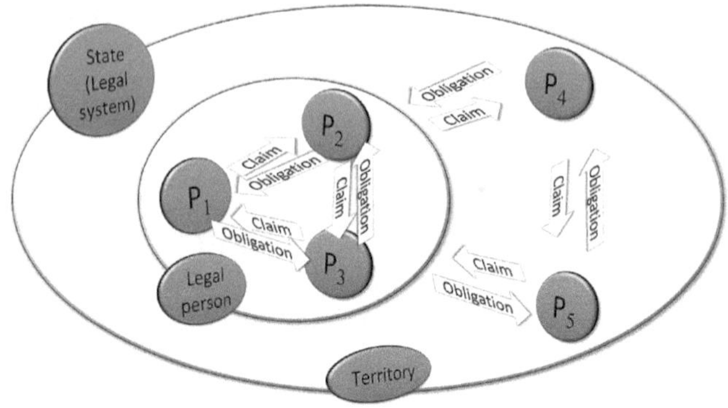

Figure 3.1 State (deontic system) (P—P—P)

international obligations via contracts with other States and non-State persons $\left(St_{\rightarrow contract\leftarrow}St(P)_{\rightarrow}St—St(P)\right)$.[22]

As we have seen,[23] States may have limited existence in time for different reasons, whereby extinction can take place based on events such as merger or dissolution, thus shaping States as 'momentary' legal systems $\left(t_1 \rightarrow t_2\right)$.[24]

3.2 International organisations as legal persons, normative systems and formal deontic networks

By means of treaties $\left(St_{\rightarrow treaty\leftarrow}St\right)$—also known as 'constitutive instruments'[25]—States can further aggregate and establish international (or intergovernmental) organisations as independent legal entities endowed with legal personality (IO: St=St),[26] which may at times also include other international organisations and non-State entities (IO: St=St=IO=P).[27] Given that they aggregate States, international organisations exercise sovereign power (*imperium*: IO_{sov}) through their organs (IO_P) as determined in the constitutive instrument (treaty), both internally and externally, that is, internationally (article 6 of the Vienna Convention on the Law of Treaties between States

22 Muir Watt, *Private International Law and Public Law*, 2015, Vol. I, at 86.

23 Section 1.4.

24 Kelsen, *General Theory*, 1945, at 219–220.

25 *Legality of the Use by a State of Nuclear Weapons in Armed Conflict (Advisory Opinion)* [1996] ICJ Reports 66, at 74– 75, para. 19.

26 *Reparation for Injuries Suffered in the Service of the United Nations (Advisory Opinion)* [1949] ICJ Reports 174, at 178–179; *Interpretation of the Agreement of 25 March 1951 between the WHO and Egypt (Advisory Opinion)* [1950] ICJ Reports 73.

27 ILC, Report on the Work of Its Sixty-Third Session (2011) *ILC Yearbook* 1, at 49, Responsibility of international organizations, article 2.

and International Organizations or between international Organizations (VCLTIO)).[28]

International organisations can be created for different purposes. Thus, through a conference held in San Francisco from 25 April to 26 June 1945, States prepared and adopted the Charter of the United Nations (UN).[29] This established the UN as an international organisation, with the fundamental aim of ensuring peace and respect for fundamental rights (preamble). Within such a context, the organisation operates through various organs $\left(t_1 \rightarrow t_7\right)$, whereby the General Assembly (UN_{GA}) is a universal body with general competence (t_1: UN Charter article 10); the Economic and Social Council (UN_{ECOSOC}) makes recommendations on economic, social, cultural, educational, health and human rights matters (t_1: UN Charter article 62); the Security Council (UN_{SC}) has primary responsibility for maintaining and restoring international peace and security (t_4: UN Charter article 24 and chapters VI and VII); and the ICJ (UN_{ICJ}) acts as the main judicial organ, delivering advisory opinions on international legal matters and deciding disputes $\left(St(IO)_{\rightarrow breach}\right)$ consensually submitted by States (t_4: ICJ Statute articles 92 and 96).

The World Trade Organization (WTO) was established through the Marrakesh Agreement[30] in 1994 and provides an institutional framework for adopting and implementing regulation in commercial matters $\left(t_1 \rightarrow t_2\right)$, with the aim of achieving free trade among State parties ($WTO_{MStP \rightarrow frtr \leftarrow PMSt}WTO$, Marrakesh Agreement article 2). The main administrative organ is the General Council (WTO_{GC}, Marrakesh Agreement article 4(2-4)), which comprises all WTO members and operationalises the different WTO agreements through several councils, committees and working groups, such as the Council for Trade in Goods, the Council for Trade in Services and the Council for Trade-Related Aspects of Intellectual Property Rights (Marrakesh Agreement article 4(5)). The different committees and working groups operate under the supervision of the Trade Policy Review Body, which reports to the General Council (Marrakesh Agreement article 4(4): $TPRB_{\rightarrow rep \rightarrow}GC$ (figure 3.2)).

The WTO system is particularly meaningful as an example of a deontic network because, besides law-making institutions, it includes a complete procedural mechanism $\left(P_{\rightarrow(no)act\rightarrow}P_{\rightarrow(no)act}\right)$ for adjudicating violations of trade claims, obligations, rights and duties under the Dispute Settlement Understanding (DSU: $t_3 \rightarrow t_7$).[31] The procedure provides that, if a controversy between WTO members concerning the violation $\left(MSt_1(IO_1)_{\rightarrow breach}\right)$ of an

28 See *Legality of the Use by a State of Nuclear Weapons* [1996] at 78, para. 25.

29 Opened for signature 26 June 1945, 1 UN Treaty Series 16, entered into force 24 October 1945.

30 Opened for signature 15 April 1994, 1867 UN Treaty Series 154, entered into force 1 January 1995.

31 See C. Mavroidis, *The WTO Dispute Settlement System: How, Why and Where?* Edward Elgar, 2022.

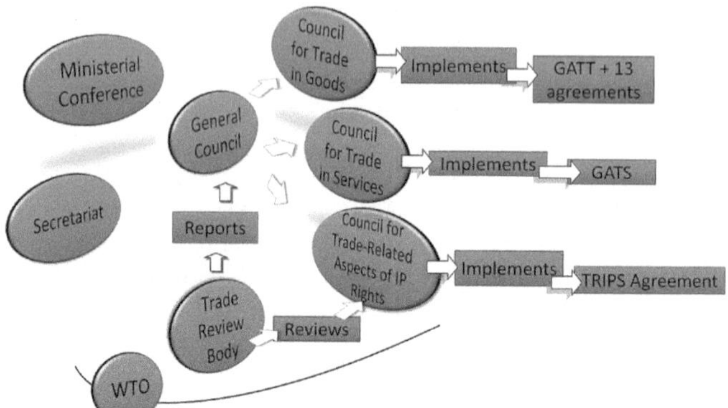

Figure 3.2 World Trade Organization

obligation or a duty $\left(MSt_1(IO_1) - ({}_2IO)_2MSt\right)$ under a convention included in the WTO umbrella cannot be settled via consultation, upon a request by the complaining party, the General Committee sitting as the Dispute Settlement Body (DSB: WTO_{DSB}) establishes a Panel $\left(DSB_{\rightarrow est \rightarrow} Pan\right)$ including independent governmental and non-governmental experts dealing with the controversy (DSU articles 6 and 8). The Panel considers the case and reports to the DSB $\left(Pan_{\rightarrow rep \rightarrow} DSB\right)$ within six months (DSU article 12(8)). The DSB further adopts the report within 60 days, unless opposite consensus is expressed or an appeal is filed by the parties with the Appellate Body (DSU article 16(4): $MSt(IO)_{\rightarrow app \rightarrow} AB\big)$, which is established by the DSB, comprises seven authoritative members appointed for four years (DSU article 17) and endorses, upholds, modifies or reverses the Panel report within a maximum time lapse of 60 days (DSU article 17(5): $AB_{\rightarrow rep \rightarrow} DSB$). Subsequently, the DSB adopts the report of the Panel or of the Appellate Body within 30 days $\left(DSB_{\rightarrow rep}\right)$, unless contrary consensus is expressed (DSU article 17(14)), whereby the overall time elapsing from the establishment of the Panel by the DSB to the date when the DSB assesses the Panel or Appellate Body report for adoption cannot exceed 9 and 12 months respectively (DSU article 20). When a report concludes that a measure is inconsistent with a duty or an obligation under a WTO treaty, sanctions $\left(MSt_1(IO_1) — ({}_2IO)_2MSt\right)$ entail mainly cessation of unlawful conduct (WTO DSU article 19(1): $MSt_1\left(IO_1\right)_{\rightarrow cess}$) and limitation or improvement of rights and obligations (WTO DSU article 19(2)). If sanctions are not performed within a reasonable time lapse, equivalent compensation and retaliatory suspension of concessions follow (DSU article 22: $MSt_1\left(IO_1\right)_{\leftarrow counterm \leftarrow 2} MSt({}_2IO)$: figure 3.3).

While most international organisations are established without time restrictions, some are only established for a limited time lapse $\left(t_1 \rightarrow t_2\right)$, as in

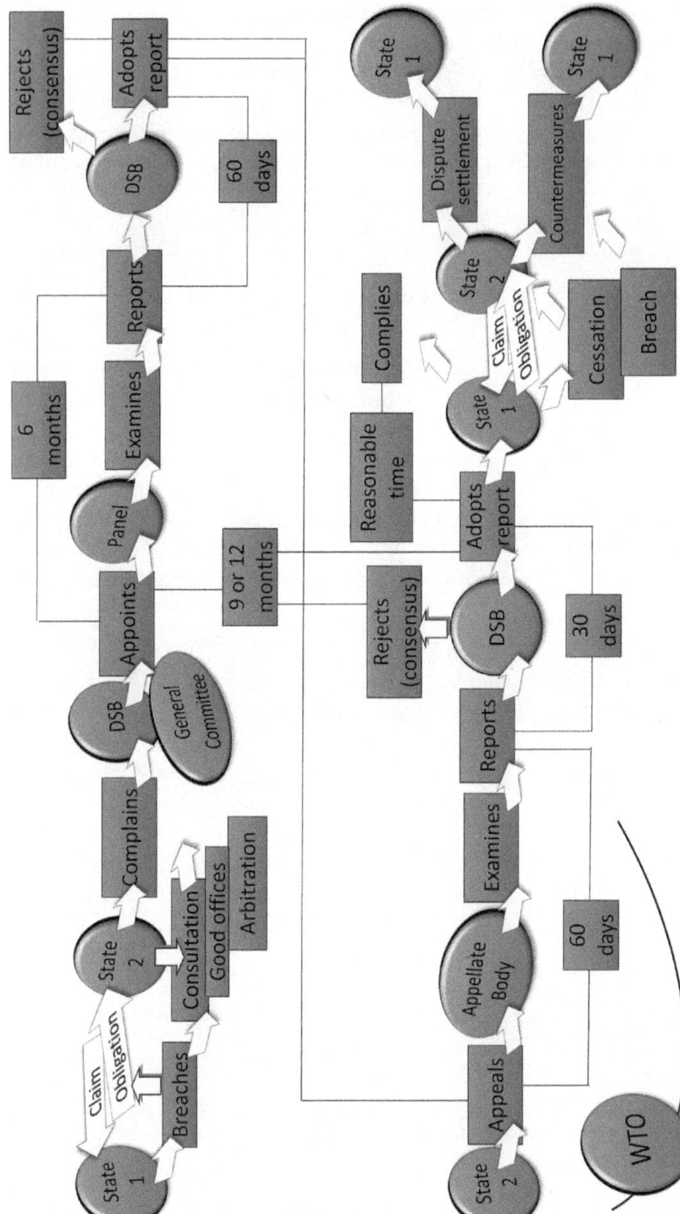

Figure 3.3 WTO dispute settlement procedure

the case of article 97 of the Treaty Establishing the European Coal and Steel Community (ECSC).[32] Furthermore, the dissolution of an international organisation can take place under different conditions, by means, for example, of a decision of the governing bodies by majority vote, as stated in article 6(5)(b) of the Articles of Agreement of the International Bank for Reconstruction and Development (IBRD).[33] Absent specific provisions, it is considered that dissolution can be imposed by the highest representative organ of an international organisation, at least via qualified majority $\left(IO_{P(qm)\rightarrow diss}\right)$,[34] which happened in the case of the dissolution of the League of Nations.[35]

3.3 International claims, obligations, rights, duties and procedures

Under 'public' international law, general (*erga omnes*) international duties, such as the freedom of the high seas, bind a State or an international organisation vis-à-vis all other sovereign persons, implying correlated claims $(St_1(IO_1)–(IO_{2,3...})St_{2,3...})$.[36] By further considering non-sovereign persons, a general international duty, such as the prohibition of genocide, binds a sovereign or non-sovereign person vis-à-vis all other sovereign and non-sovereign persons in the international legal order, entailing correlated claims $\left(P_1 - P_{2,3...}\right)$.[37] *Erga omnes* duties (and rights) are fundamentally grounded in customary procedures $\left(t_1\text{: } St(IO)_{\rightarrow custom\leftarrow}(IO)St\right)$, as codified in ICJ Statute article 38(1)(a) and in article 26 of the Vienna Convention on the Law of Treaties (VCLT) and of the VCLTIO: *consuetudo est servanda* $\left(St_{1,2...}(IO_{1,2...}) - (IO_{3,4...})St_{3,4...}\right)$.[38] Among such norms, peremptory duties are indivisible and cannot thus be derogated from bilaterally and multilaterally, as outlined in article 53 of the VCLT and VCLTIO and further spelled out by international courts as concerns both sovereign and non-sovereign persons.[39] Peremptory norms

32 Opened for signature 18 April 1951, 261 UN Treaty Series 140, entered into force 23 July 1952, expired 23 July 2002.

33 Opened for signature 22 July 1944, 2 UN Treaty Series 39, entered into force 27 December 1945.

34 F. Amerasinghe, *Principles of Institutional Law of International Organisations*, Cambridge University Press, 2nd ed., 2005, at 468–469.

35 Assembly of the League of Nations, Resolution for the Dissolution of the League of Nations, 18 April 1946.

36 See, for instance, Y. Tanaka, 'The Legal Consequences of Obligations *Erga Omnes* in International Law' (2021) 68(1) *Netherlands International Law Review* 1, at 3.

37 Tanaka, 'The Legal Consequences of Obligations', at 6.

38 Tanaka, 'The Legal Consequences of Obligations', at 3.

39 *Barcelona Traction, Light and Power Company, Limited (New Application: 1962) (Belgium v. Spain) Second Phase (Judgment)* [1970] ICJ Reports 3, at 32, paras. 33–34; *Furundžija*, IT-95–17/1, Trial Chamber, Judgment of 10 December 1998, at 58–59, paras 153–154.

(*ius cogens*) therefore establish a static (Leibnizian) hierarchical (vertical ↑↓) order between international rights and duties.[40] By contrast, particular international obligations and duties, such as the most-favoured-nation (MFN) clause under the General Agreement on Trade and Tariffs (GATT),[41] bind a sovereign or non-sovereign person vis-à-vis another sovereign person (bilateral obligation: $St_1(IO_1)-(IO_2)St_2$) or vis-à-vis some sovereign persons (multilateral obligations: relative duty $St_1(IO_1)-(IO_{2,3...})St_{2,3...}$).[42] Particular obligations, duties, claims and rights are essentially grounded in agreements $\left(t_1\text{: } St(IO)_{\rightarrow \text{treaty} \leftarrow}(IO)St\right)$ as established in ICJ Statute article 38(1)(b) and in VCLT and VCLTIO article 26: *pacta sunt servanda* $\left(St_{1,2...}(IO_{1,2...})-(IO_{3,4...})St_{3,4...}\right)$.[43]

Horizontally, when a primary international obligation—claim $\left(St_1(IO_1)-(IO_2)St_2\right)$ and duty—right $\left(St_1(IO_1)-(IO_{2,3...})St_{2,3...}\right)$ relationship (1) linking sovereign entities is breached $\left(t_3\text{: } St_1\,(IO_1)_{\rightarrow \text{breach}}\right)$, the application of a sanction $\left(t_5\text{: } St_1(IO_1)-(IO_{2,3\,...})\,St_{2,3...}\right)$ takes place via invocation of responsibility by the injured State or international organisation and also by non-injured States and international organisations $\left(St_{2,3...}(IO_{2,3...})_{\rightarrow \text{invoc}}\right)$ in the case of indivisible *erga omnes* duties (*ius cogens*), as codified in articles 42, 46 and 48 of the ILC's Draft Articles on State Responsibility (DASR) and in articles 43, 47 and 49 of the ILC's Draft Articles on the Responsibility of International Organizations (DARIO), or via the submission of the breach to negotiation, mediation, conciliation, arbitration and judicial dispute settlement (t_4) (DASR 56, DARIO 65 and UN Charter articles 33–38).[44] If an obligation—claim $\left(St_1(IO_1)-(IO_2)St_2\right)$ or duty—right $\left(St_1(IO_1)-(IO_{2,3...})St_{2,3...}\right)$ relationship imposed as a sanction (2), notably involving cessation and reparation, between sovereign entities is breached $\left(t_6\text{: } St_1(IO_1)_{\rightarrow \text{breach}}\right)$, enforcement ($t_7$) is implemented via countermeasures adopted by one, some (divisible duties) or all (indivisible duties) States independently (DASR article 49: $St_1\left(IO_1\right)_{\leftarrow \text{counterm} \leftarrow ...3,2}St$) or via procedures institutionalised through international organisations (DARIO article 51: $St_1\left(IO_1\right)_{\leftarrow \text{counterm} \leftarrow ...,3,2}IO$). For instance, if the primary duty not to resort to armed force $\left(t_2\text{: } St_1(IO_1)-(IO_{2,3...})St_{2,3.}\right)$ under UN Charter article 2(4)

40 D. Shelton, *Jus Cogens*, Oxford University Press, 2024, at 102.

41 Opened for signature 30 October 1947, 55 UN Treaty Series 194, entered into force 1 June 1948.

42 Kelsen, *Principles of International Law*, 1952, at 288.

43 Kelsen, *General Theory*, 1945, at 369; T. Christiano, 'The Legitimacy of International Institutions', in A. Marmor (ed.), *The Routledge Companion to Philosophy of Law*, Routledge, 2012, 380, at 384.

44 See further, E. De Brabandere, 'International Adjudication and Jurisdictional Conflict', in U. Linderfalk (ed.), *The International Legal System as a System of Knowledge*, Edward Elgar, 2021, 182.

and customary international law (t_1)[45] is breached by a State $(t_3\text{: }St_{1\rightarrow breach})$, cessation and reparation $(t_5\text{: }St_1 - St_{2,3...}(IO_{2,3...}))$ may be invoked by the injured State(s) or international organisation(s) and also by non-injured States and international organisations, as this is an indivisible *erga omnes* duty (*ius cogens*) $(t_4\text{: }St_{2,3...}(IO_{2,3...})_{\rightarrow invoc})$, and, if the breach is not settled amicably, the sanction $(St_1 - (IO_{2,3...})St_{2,3...})$ will be imposed by international courts seized by means of interstate agreements or through UN procedures (t_4). Eventually, if the injurer does not cease unlawful conduct and provide compensation, thus violating (t_6) the secondary duty imposed as a sanction $(t_5\text{: }St_{1\rightarrow breach})$, the injured State(s) and also non-injured States, as this is an indivisible *erga omnes* duty (*ius cogens*), will be able to adopt counter-measures such as resorting to armed force, triggering the law of war,[46] and confiscating property, which can also be institutionalised via international organisations $(t_7\text{: }St_{1\leftarrow counterm\leftarrow ...,3,2}St(_{...3,2}IO))$.

It is thus clear that the norms embedded in the VCLT, VCLTIO, DASR and DARIO provide a comprehensive codification of international law. The VCLT and VCLTIO govern primary procedural rules on the sources of international law $(t_1\text{: }St(IO)_{\rightarrow treaty/custom\leftarrow}(IO)St)$, notably treaties and ensuing claims, rights, obligations and duties $(t_2\text{: }St_{1,2...}(IO_{1,2...}) - (IO_{3,4...})St_{3,4...})$. For example, VCLT and VCLTIO article 11 (Means of Expressing Consent to be Bound by a Treaty) is a procedural rule $(t_1\text{: }St(IO)_{\rightarrow treaty\leftarrow}(IO)St)$, whereas article 42 (Validity and Continuance in Force of Treaties) governs ensuing substantive claim—obligation and right—duty relationships $(t_2\text{: }St_{1,2...}(IO_{1,2...}) - (IO_{3,4...}St_{3,4...})$. By contrast, the DASR and DARIO are concerned with secondary rules. Thus, DASR part 1 and DARIO part 2 (Internationally Wrongful Act of a State or an International Organisation) embed substantive rules focusing on conduct that is inconsistent with an international obligation $(t_3\text{: liability }St_{1,2...}(IO_{1,2...})_{\rightarrow breach})$. DASR part 2 and DARIO part 3 (Content of the International Responsibility of a State or an International Organisation) govern secondary sanctions following the violation of a primary obligation or duty (t_5: secondary obligation—claim (duty—right) relationships $St_{1,2...}(IO_{1,2...}) - (IO_{3,4...})St_{3,4...}$), including cessation and reparation $(St_{1,2...}(IO_{1,2...})_{\rightarrow cess/rep})$. DASR part 3 and DARIO part 4 (Implementation of the International Responsibility of a State or an International Organisation) embed procedural rules on invocation of responsibility $(t_4\text{: dispute settlement: }St_{3,4...}(IO_{3,4...})_{\rightarrow invoc})$, infringement of the

45 *Military and Paramilitary Activities in and against Nicaragua (Nicaragua v. United States of America) (Judgment)* [1986] ICJ Reports 14, at 99, para. 188.

46 See Grotius, *De jure belli ac pacis*, 1625, at 15.

sanction $\left(t_6\text{: liability } St_{1,2...}(IO_{1,2...})_{\rightarrow breach}\right)$ and countermeasures $\left(t_7\text{: enforcement } St_{1,2...}(IO_{1,2...})_{\leftarrow counterm\leftarrow ...4,3}St(_{...4,3}IO)\right)$.

As concerns natural persons, some international treaties $\left(t_1\text{: } St(IO)_{\rightarrow treaty\leftarrow}(IO)St\right)$ directly regulate international offences $\left(P_{1,2...} - P_{3,4...}\text{: } t_2 \rightarrow t_3\right)$ and ensuing procedures $\left(t_4 \rightarrow t_7\right)$. For example, the Rome Statute of the International Criminal Court (ICC)[47] prohibits international crimes and creates a supranational jurisdiction (IO_P) with competence over them. The ICC is the result of a historical process that commenced with the creation of the International Military Tribunals in Nuremberg and Tokyo after World War II[48] and continued with other *ad hoc* tribunals such as the International Criminal Tribunal for the Former Yugoslavia and the International Criminal Tribunal for Rwanda in the 1990s.[49] The establishment of international jurisdictions (t_4: dispute settlement procedures) overcomes the obstacle of the immunity of natural persons. Secondary duties or sanctions $\left(t_5\text{: } P_{1,2...} - P_{3,4...}\right)$ imposing imprisonment, fines and reparation through judgments of supranational criminal jurisdictions $\left(t_4 : IO_{P\rightarrow decision}\right)$, however, are enforced by States domestically under national procedures $\left(t_6 \rightarrow t_7\text{: } St_{\rightarrow enforc}\right)$ in a cooperative context (figure 3.4).

Under 'private' international law, transboundary legal relationships $\left(t_2\text{: } P—P\right)$, involving both sovereign and non-sovereign persons,[50] are governed through contracts $\left(t_1\text{: } P_{\rightarrow prop—acc\leftarrow}P\right)$, whereby persons act *more privatorum*, outside the exercise of sovereign power. For example, this happens when two or more persons based in different States conclude a contract for sale of goods, which is harmonised within the framework of the VCCISG (article 1). If a primary obligation $\left(P_1 - P_2\right)$ is then breached $\left(P_{1\rightarrow breach}\right)$, the substance of the breach (t_3), dispute resolution (t_4), ensuing sanctions $\left(P_1 - P_2\right)$, notably imposing specific performance $\left(t_5\text{: } P_{1\rightarrow spperf}\right)$, and enforcement procedures $\left(t_6 \rightarrow t_7\text{: } P_{1\leftarrow enf\leftarrow 2}P\right)$ are governed via international conventions and applicable domestic law, based on conflict of laws principles, such as the choice of the parties or the place where the cause of action arises: that is, *lex situs* or *lex loci* (*actus*, *contractus*, *commissi delicti*, *solutionis*).[51] Applicable dispute

47 Opened for signature 27 July 1998, 2187 UN Treaty Series 2, entered into force 1 July 2002.

48 Charter of the International Military Tribunal, Nuremberg, adopted 8 August 1945; Charter of the International Military Tribunal for the Far East, Tokyo, adopted 19 January 1946.

49 UN Security Council, Establishment of the International Criminal Tribunal for the Former Yugoslavia, Resolution 827/1993; UN Security Council, Establishment of the International Criminal Tribunal for Rwanda, Resolution 955/1994.

50 *Payment of Various Serbian Loans Issued in France (France v. Serbia) (Judgment)* [1929] PCIJ Series A No. 20, 3, at 41.

51 See the 1980 Rome Convention on the Law Applicable to Contractual Obligations, opened for signature 19 June 1980, 19 International Legal Materials 1492, entered into force 1 April 1991 and the 2007 Rome II Regulation on the Law Applicable to Non-contractual Obligations

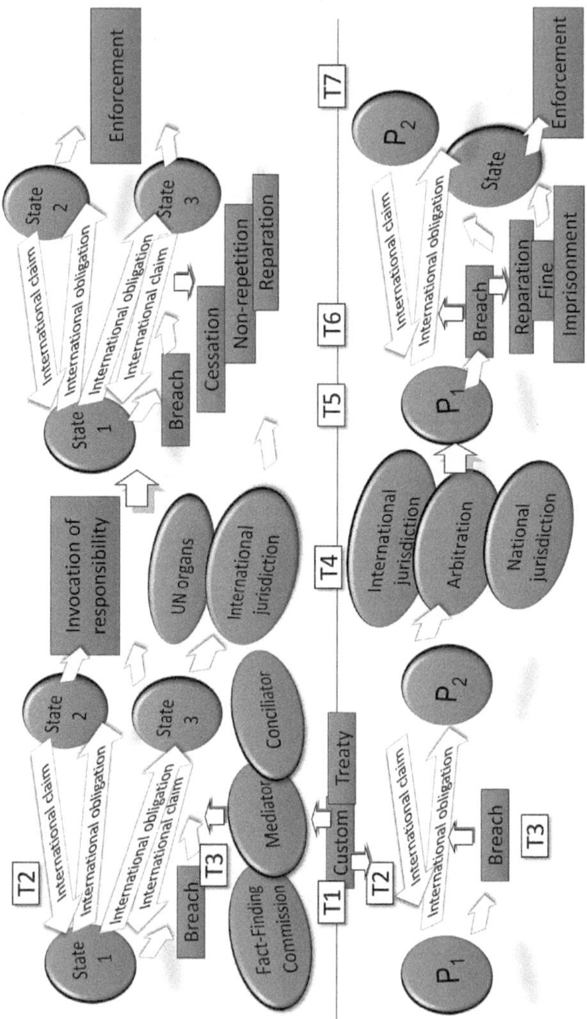

Figure 3.4 'Public' international law (and procedure)

resolution means include consultation (negotiation), arbitration and adjudication (t_4). Thus, for example, the case of *Vita Food Products Inc.* was concerned with a bill of lading concluded between a shipowner in Canada and a consignee in New York (Shipowner—Consignee) to deliver herring, whereby a ship ran aground, and the consignment was damaged. The consignee sued the shipowner for negligence in Canada, but the defendant validly invoked the exemption defence under English law, given that the parties had singled out the law of England as the applicable law, overriding clauses from Canadian and US law.[52] In *Texaco Overseas Petroleum Company*, an international arbitrator decided upon the nationalisation by Libya of the rights, interests and property of Texaco Overseas Petroleum Company and California Asiatic Oil Company, revoking 14 Deeds of Concession between 1973 and 1974.[53] The sole arbitrator of the dispute held Libya in violation of the concessions (Libya—Texaco & Calasiatic) in light of the principles of Libyan law, consistent with the principles of international law and the general principles of law.[54] As a follow-up to decisions imposing sanctions (P—P), instruments such as the 1958 New York Convention on the Recognition and Enforcement of Foreign Arbitral Awards (CREFAA)[55] compel the parties to recognise and execute foreign and international awards $\left(St_{\rightarrow rec \rightarrow enf}\right)$, as in figure 3.5.

We can therefore conclude that international law is a regulatory system encompassing norms governing legal relationships that involve a foreign element, including interstate and transnational legal relationships.[56] As a consequence, it is possible to define international law as the whole claim—obligation (or obligation—claim) relationships that regulate behaviour (action and inaction) among legal state orders (St(IO)—(IO)St) and subjects belonging to different state orders (P—P), summarising the idea of '*ius gentium*' proposed by Scelle.[57] Ultimately, international law can be conceived of as a deontic network (St=IO=P=P) overarching state legal networks (St=P=P):[58] after all, international law can be simply visualised through

(European Parliament and EU Council, Law Applicable to Non-contractual Obligations, Regulation (EC) No. 864/2007).

52 *Vita Food Products Inc v. Unus Shipping Company Ltd.* [1939] AC 277.

53 *Texaco Overseas Petroleum Company/California Asiatic Oil Company v. the Government of the Libyan Arab Republic (Compensation for Nationalized Property)*, Award (1978) 17(1) International Legal Materials 1.

54 *Texaco Overseas Petroleum Company* (1978) at 11, para. 23.

55 Opened for signature 10 June 1958, 330 UN Treaty Series 38, entered into force 7 June 1959.

56 M.D. Varella, *Internationalization of Law: Globalization, International Law and Complexity*, Springer, 2014, at 253; O. Quirico, *The International Legal System*, Thomson Reuters, 2020, at 80–81; A. Bostanu, 'Transnational Law: A New System of Law?' (2021) 11(special issue) *Juridical Tribune* 332.

57 G. Scelle, *Précis de droit des gens: principes et systématique*, Sirey, 1932, at 27 ff.

58 See K.H. Kawaguchi, *A Social Theory of International Law: International Relations as a Complex System*, Springer, 2003.

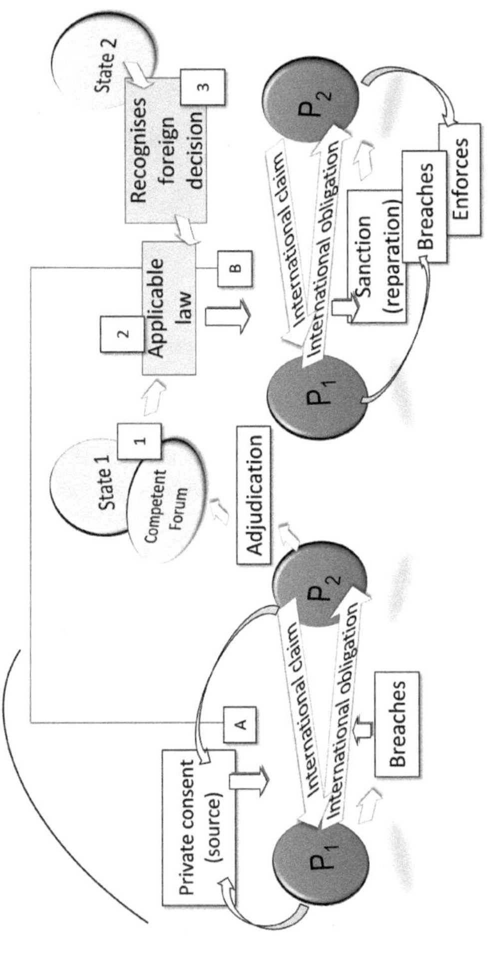

Figure 3.5 'Private' international law (and procedure)

a geopolitical world map.[59] In this context, both the normative character $\left(\mathrm{St(IO)(P)—(P)(IO)St}\right)$ of international practice $\left(\mathrm{St(IO)(P)}_{\rightarrow\mathrm{(no)act}}\right)$ and the procedural nature $\left(\mathrm{St(IO)(P)}_{\rightarrow\mathrm{(no)act(t1)}\rightarrow}\mathrm{St(IO)(P)}_{\rightarrow\mathrm{(no)(act)(t2)}}\right)$ of international legal norms $\left(\mathrm{St(IO)(P)—(P)(IO)St}\right)$ are underscored, whereby the notion of 'time' plays a key role in determining change and development.[60]

3.4 EU law as a legal person, a normative system and a formal deontic network

The EU is an international organisation with specific sovereign features, currently including 27 Member States. Historically (temporally), on 18 April 1951, France, West Germany, Italy, Belgium, Luxembourg and the Netherlands concluded the Treaty of Paris, which entered into force on 23 July 1952, establishing the ECSC (t_1), and expired 50 years later on 23 July 2002. On 25 March 1957, the Treaty Establishing the European Economic Community (TEEC)[61] and the Treaty Establishing the European Atomic Energy Community (Euratom)[62] were concluded in Rome and entered into force on 1 January 1958 (t_2). On 7 February 1992, the members of the EEC, which had by then expanded to include Denmark, Ireland and the United Kingdom (1973), Greece (1981), Spain and Portugal (1986), signed in Maastricht a treaty which entered into force on 1 November 1993 and led to creating the EU as a three-pillared structure without international legal personality, including the EC—now based on the Treaty on European Union (TEU)[63] and the TEC (former TEEC)—Common Foreign and Security Policy (CFSP) and Police and Judicial Cooperation in Criminal Matters (PJCC) (t_3). After the rejection of the Constitution for Europe, following the negative outcome of the referendums held in France and the Netherlands in 2005 (t_4),[64] the Lisbon Treaty was adopted in 2009,[65] including the revised TEU, the Treaty on the Functioning of the EU (TFEU, former TEC) and the Charter of Fundamental Rights of the European Union, establishing the EU as an international legal person (P) resulting from the fusion of the three pillars created via the

59 See, for instance, A. Bautzmann, *Atlals géopolitique mondial*, Rocher, 2024.

60 Van der Ploeg, 'International Law through Time' (2022) at 316 and 318.

61 Opened for signature 25 March 1957, 298 UN Treaty Series 3, entered into force 1 January 1958.

62 Opened for signature 25 March 1957, 298 UN Treaty Series 259, entered into force 1 January 1958.

63 Opened for signature 7 February 1992, 31 International Legal Materials 247, entered into force 1 November 1993.

64 Treaty Establishing a Constitution for Europe, 29 October 2004.

65 Treaty of Lisbon Amending the Treaty on European Union and the Treaty Establishing the European Community, opened for signature 13 December 2007, 2702 UN Treaty Series 3 No. 47938, entered into force 1 December 2009.

Maastricht Treaty (t_5). Such developments in the primary sources of EU law demonstrate that the EEC was initially aimed at creating a common market—that is, a free trade area between Member States $\left(EU_{MStP \rightarrow frtr \leftarrow PMSt} EU\right)$[66]—but has evolved to achieve broader political objectives, including a common foreign policy and fundamental rights promotion. On 1 February 2020, the UK ceased to be a Member of the Union (t_6).[67]

The (hierarchically ↑↓) primary sources of EU law establish the Union as an international organisation (EU: MSt=MSt), whereby the European Council (EU_{EC}), the Commission (EU_{Com}), the Council of the EU (EU_C), the Parliament (EU_{Par}) and the Court of Justice of the EU (EU_{CJEU}) are the main regulatory organs mandated to adopt and apply (hierarchically ↑↓) secondary EU law $\left(t_1 \rightarrow t_7\right)$ (TEU article 13). More specifically, the Councils, the Parliament and the Commission are concerned with law-making (t_1) and thus with creating, varying and removing claim—obligation (or obligation—claim) and right—duty (or duty—right) relationships (t_2: EU—MSt, MSt—MSt, P—P) while the CJEU adjudicates breaches of primary rules ($t_3 \rightarrow t_4$) and thus imposes sanctions (t_5: P—P, EU—MSt, MSt—MSt). Notably, the EU institutions can only exercise legislative power (t_1) in areas where sovereignty has been explicitly transferred by the Member States (TEU article 5(2): $MSt_{\rightarrow transf \rightarrow sov} EU$); otherwise, power remains within the remit of the States (TEU article 4(1)). Moreover, the competence of EU institutions can be exclusive, shared, coordinated or complementary (TFEU article 2). In light of such an advanced normative power, the EU can be considered a specific type of international organisation, notably, a 'supranational' one.[68] Among different regulatory tools, the main binding instruments available to the EU institutions are directives, regulations and decisions. According to the 'ordinary' legislative procedure (t_1), upon initiative by the Commission $\left(EU_{Com \rightarrow init}\right)$, EU legislative acts are taken on a basis of equality between the Council and the Parliament (TFEU article 289(1): co-decision, $EU_{C,Parl \rightarrow co\text{-}dec}$), but within the framework of 'special' legislative procedures such a balance is altered (TFEU article 289(2)). As a result of legislative procedures, directives address all or specific EU Member States and bind such States $\left(t_2\text{: } EU—MSt_{1,2\ldots}—MSt_{3,4\ldots}\right)$ to further pass national legislation $\left(t_1\text{: } MSt_{\rightarrow leg}\right)$ and regulate binding domestic legal claims, obligations, rights and duties $\left(t_1\text{: } MSt—P_{1,2\ldots}—P_{3,4\ldots}\right)$. A directive therefore harmonises domestic law by outlining the basic objectives to be achieved by States, which enjoy a more or less extensive margin of discretion in implementing the ensuing duties. For instance, Directive 2003/88/EC

66 *Van Gend and Loos*, ECJ, Case 26/61, Judgment of 5 February 1963 [1963] ECR 00003.

67 Withdrawal Agreement, notified 29 March 2017, entered into force 31 January 2020.

68 See A. Lopez-Claros, A.L. Dahl and M. Groff, *Global Governance and the Emergence of Global Institutions for the 21st Century*, Cambridge University Press, 2020, 65.

outlines mandatory limits on working time authorised in EU Member States.[69] By contrast, a regulation is directly applicable within all Member States of the Union and binds all or specific categories of natural and legal persons $\left(t_{1\to}t_2\text{: EU}_{\text{Com,C,Par}\to\text{reg}\to}P_1 - P_{2,3\ldots}\right)$. For example, Regulation 1169/2011 establishes general duties on food information and labelling.[70] Decisions (t_1) are also directly applicable and binding upon or within some or all of the Member States of the EU $\left(t_{1\to}t_2\text{: EU}_{\text{Com,C,Par}\to\text{dec}\to}\text{MSt—MSt,P—P}\right)$, but only with respect to specifically targeted natural or legal persons $\left(P_1 - P_2\right)$. For instance, Decision 2016/1189 authorised Dairy Crest Ltd. to place UV-treated milk on the market as a novel food (figure 3.6).[71]

Horizontally, breaches of obligations and duties (t_3) under EU law are mainly adjudicated by domestic courts and by the CJEU (t_4), which includes the Court of Justice, the General Court and specialised courts ($\text{CJEU}_{\text{CJ,GC,SC}}$, TEU article 17 and TFEU article 251). Different proceedings can be initiated in the CJEU, depending on the plaintiff, the legal relationship at issue and the consequences of the action. Under the preliminary ruling procedure, when they have to apply EU law, any domestic courts or tribunals can stay proceedings and request the CJEU $\left(\text{St}_{\text{Court}\to\text{rec}\to}\text{EU}_{\text{CJEU}}\right)$ to explain a point of Union law via a non-contentious incidental process, whereby the Court replies by means of a judgment (t_4), ensuring a uniform interpretation of EU law throughout domestic jurisdictions $\left(\text{CJEU}_{\to(\text{int})\text{judg}}\right)$, with EU law overriding

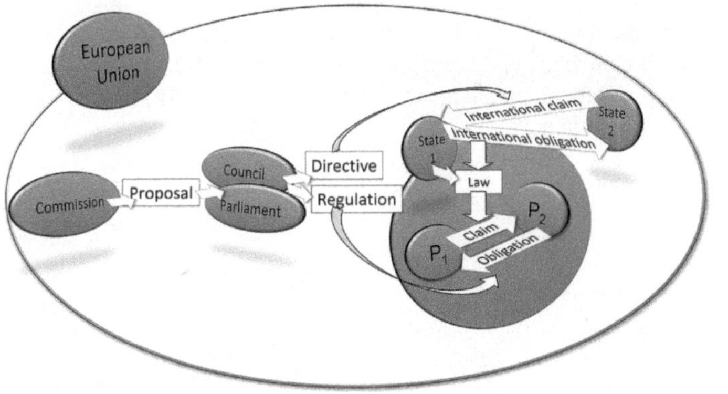

Figure 3.6 EU (vertical) law-making

69 European Parliament and Council, Directive 2003/88/EC of 4 November 2003 Concerning Certain Aspects of the Organisation of Working Time, 299 OJ L 9.

70 European Parliament and Council, Regulation of 25 October 2011 on the Provision of Food Information to Consumers, Doc. 02011R1169-20140219.

71 European Commission, Implementing Decision (EU) 2016/1189 of 19 July 2016 Authorising the Placing on the Market of UV-treated Milk as a Novel Food under Regulation (EC) No. 258/97 of the European Parliament and of the Council, 196 OJ L 50.

(>) national law (TFEU article 267). Action for treaty infringement initiated by the Commission (TFEU article 258: $EU_{Com \to rec \to}CJEU$) or by a Member State (TFEU article 259: $MSt_{\to rec \to}CJEU$) aims to determine whether an EU Member State fails to fulfil $(MSt_{\to breach})$ an obligation arising from the founding treaties $(t_2 \to t_4$: MSt—EU, MSt—MSt$)$—for instance, because of a failure to transpose a directive of the Union—and can lead to imposing sanctions on a Member State in order to bring its conduct into conformity with treaty obligations $(t_5$: MSt—EU, MSt—MSt$)$. If a Member State fails to comply with a court's decision $(t_6: MSt_{\to breach})$, the Commission has the possibility of obtaining a second court ruling enjoining that State to undergo a lump-sum fine or a penalty $(t_7$: MSt—EU, MSt—MSt, TFEU article 260$)$. Action for annulment under TFEU article 263 allows EU citizens, Member States, the European Parliament, the Council, the Commission, the Court of Auditors, the European Central Bank and the Committee of the Regions to lodge with the CJEU requests for annulment $(t_4: MSt, P, EU_{Par,C,CA,CR,ECB \to rec \to}CJEU)$ of acts taken by EU institutions $(EU_{P \to act})$ infringing their rights $(t_3: EU - MSt_{2,3...,}P_{4,5...,}EP, EC, CR)$. If the action succeeds, the CJEU may declare an EU legal act void with retroactive (←) or non-retroactive (→) effect $(t_5: EU - MSt_{2,3...,}P_{4,5...,}EP, EC, CR)$. A complaint for failure to act under TFEU article 265 provides the same plaintiffs with the possibility of putting an EU institution on notice to fulfil its duty $(EU - MSt_{2,3...,}P_{4,5...,}EP, EC, CR)$ and, in the case of a failure $(t_3: EU_{P \to no\text{-}act})$, to commence proceedings in the CJEU $(t_4: MSt, P, EU_{Par,C,CR,ECB \to rec \to}CJEU)$ to declare that EU institutions have infringed the founding treaties by failing to adopt a compulsory decision (t_3). As a follow-up to action for annulment and failure to act, the CJEU can enjoin the EU institutions to take action $(t_5: MSt_{2,3...,}P_{4,5...,}EP, EC, CR - EU_{P \to act})$ under TFEU article 266.

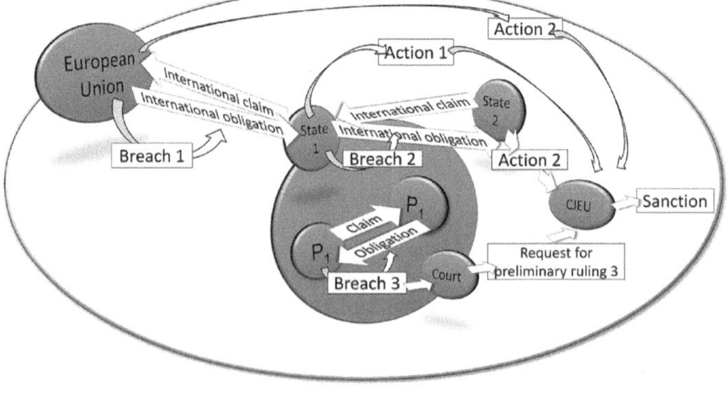

Figure 3.7 EU (horizontal) dispute settlement procedures

Under action for damage outlined in TFEU articles 268 and 340(2), citizens, legal entities and Member States that suffer damages because of the conduct of EU staff $\left(t_3\text{: } EU_{P\rightarrow breach}\right)$ can enter proceedings in the CJEU $\left(t_4\text{: } MSt_{\rightarrow rec\rightarrow}CJEU\right)$, provided that actual damage is sufficiently serious, exceeding the limits of discretionary power to a considerable degree, and a causal link is proven between EU conduct and sustained damage $\left(EU_P - P{,}MSt\right)$.

3.5 Unlimited spatial (and temporal) extension of deontic networks: universality?

The question of the (finite or indefinite) extension of the law in space (and time) has not attracted much attention in scholarly work. The issue has been approached particularly from a monistic perspective, considering that international law has an indefinite sphere (•) of validity in space and time as a consequence of the fact that, unlike the State itself, which has limited territorial and temporal effectiveness, international law would not be subject to any superior sovereign authority.[72] International law would therefore expand together with the universe (•). Indeed, there is no norm in international law or outside it superior to international rules that might limit the effectiveness of international law in either time or space.[73] This would hold true regardless of whether international law effectively regulates conduct in any part of the universe, notably outside the jurisdiction of States, and would apply particularly to the general rules of international law, specifically the norm '*pacta sunt servanda*' $\left(St_{1,2...}(IO_{1,2...}) - (IO_{3,4...})St_{3,4...}\right)$.[74]

However, it has to be noted that most spaces on Earth and in outer space are not subject to jurisdiction. Indeed, beyond the limits of the territorial sea (12 nautical miles from a State's coast baseline) and of atmospheric space (around 62 miles above sea level), the concept of jurisdiction fades. Deontic networks therefore appear as intensive 'regulatory clusters' in sovereign spaces and as 'low-level regulatory clusters' outside the boundaries of full sovereignty.[75] Nonetheless, low-level normative clusters do not emerge from empty regulatory spaces as, if there were space where no rules apply (Bentham's negative society), this would fundamentally coincide with the mono-normative system where all is permitted—the Hobbesian *bellum omnium contra omnes*—which is the minimum possible extension of regulatory networks.[76] Furthermore,

72 Kelsen, *Principles of International Law*, 1952, at 93–94.

73 Kelsen, *Principles of International Law*, 1952, at 93–94. But, for a dualistic perspective, see G.W.F Hegel, *Philosophie des Geistes (Philosophy of Mind)*, tr. W. Wallace and A.V. Miller, Clarendon Press, 2007, at 246, para. 547.

74 Kelsen, *Principles of International Law*, 1952, at 95–96.

75 See G.M. Danilenko, 'International Law-Making for Outer Space' (2016) 37 *Space Policy* 179.

76 See s. 2.1.

currently this is not the case as, when natural or legal persons venture on the high seas or in outer space, claims, obligations, rights and duties are 'extended' with a low level of intensity but not the minimum one in which all is permitted, given that such spaces are subject to the fundamental obligation of use in the common interest of all (Outer Space Treaty article 1; UNCLOS article 88). Moreover, specific rules apply, such as the duty not to put into orbit objects carrying nuclear weapons or weapons of mass destruction under Outer Space Treaty article 4. In this context, the geostationary orbit, which is located 22,236 miles directly above the equator, emerges as a notable example of normativity (P—P) applying in outer space. Indeed, based on gravitation, on the geostationary orbit, satellites circle at the same speed following the Earth's rotation, allowing motionless communication between antennae on Earth and satellites on the orbit. In 1976, this feature prompted Brazil, Colombia, Congo, Ecuador, Indonesia, Kenya, Uganda and Zaire to adopt a declaration to the effect that 'the segments of the geostationary synchronous orbit are part of the territory over which equatorial States exercise their sovereignty'.[77] However, the declaration has given rise to objections and disputes over allocation of the geostationary orbit are to be resolved via the International Telecommunication Union.[78]

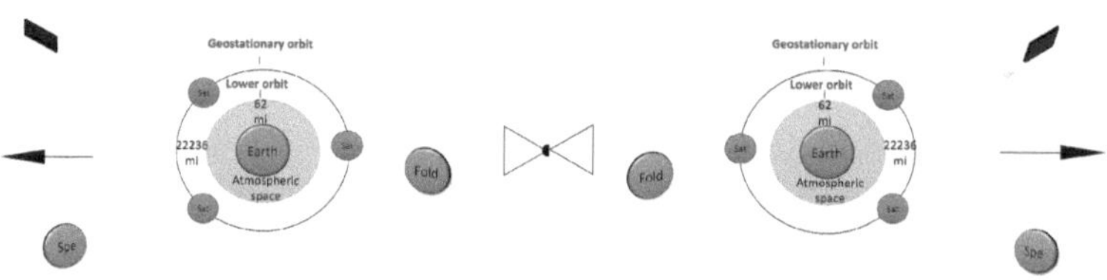

Figure 3.8 Space-time: universe(s)

More fundamentally, there are different theories in physics according to which space and time might be organised following different laws in the universe, which obviously relativises the applicability of deontic networks grounded in the idea of linear procedures. Thus, in the world where we live, after the Big Bang, time is considered to flow from the past to the present and future as an arrow, whereby, following the second law of thermodynamics, our universe started as an infinitesimally small dot (•) 13.8 billion years ago and

77 Declaration of the First Meeting of Equatorial Countries, 3 December 1976, s. 1.

78 See L. Roberts, 'A Lost Connection: Geostationary Satellite Networks and the International Telecommunication Union' (2000) 15(3) *Berkeley Technology Law Journal* 1095, at 1112.

has since been expanding from order (low entropy) to disorder (high entropy): no person grows old to young.[79] However, other suggestions have been put forward, compelling a revision of the idea of the arrow of time, including the view that the Big Bang would not be a simple starting point in time flowing from the past towards the present and future, but rather a midpoint generating two mirror universes, with time flowing in opposite directions.[80]

79 Barbour, *The End of Time*, 2001, at 23.

80 See A. Einstein, H.A. Lorentz, H. Weil and H. Minkowski, *The Principle of Relativity: A Collection of Original Memoirs on the Special and General Theory of Relativity*, Methuen, 1923; P. Merriam, 'A Theory of the Big Bang in McTaggart's Time' (2022) 32(suppl 3) *Axiomathes* S685; J. Barbour, *The Janus Point: A New Theory of Time*, Basic Books, 2020; A. Campo and S. Gozzano, *Einstein vs. Bergson: An Enduring Quarrel on Time*, De Gruyter, 2022.

Conclusion

The law as a formal deontic network

A norm can be conceived of as a (network of) claim—obligation (or right—duty) relationship(s) (1) that regulate(s) conduct (action or inaction) (2) among persons (3), in space (4(sp)(•)) and time (5(t → t)).

This can be expressed via Kripke-style semantics (social matrix) and further translated into iconic graph-theoretic notation.

$$\boldsymbol{Norm} =_{\mathrm{p1,(p3)}} \boldsymbol{Claim}\ \mathrm{(NON)A} - \mathrm{(NON)A}\ \boldsymbol{Obl}_{\mathrm{p2,(p4)space/time}}$$

$$\boldsymbol{Right}_{\mathrm{p1}}\mathrm{(NON)A} - \boldsymbol{Obl}_{\mathrm{p2,p3}}\mathrm{(NON)A}$$

$$\boldsymbol{Right}_{\mathrm{p2}}\mathrm{(NON)A} - \boldsymbol{Obl}_{\mathrm{p1,p3}}\mathrm{(NON)A}$$

$$\boldsymbol{Right}_{\mathrm{p3}}\mathrm{(NON)A} - \boldsymbol{Obl}_{\mathrm{p1,p2}}\mathrm{(NON)A}$$

$$\boldsymbol{Claim}_{\mathrm{p2,p3}}\ \mathrm{(NON)A} - \boldsymbol{Duty}_{\mathrm{p1}}\ \mathrm{(NON)A}$$

$$\boldsymbol{Claim}_{\mathrm{p1,p3}}\ \mathrm{(NON)A} - \boldsymbol{Duty}_{\mathrm{p2}}\ \mathrm{(NON)A}$$

$$\boldsymbol{Claim}_{\mathrm{p1,p2}}\ \mathrm{(NON)A} - \boldsymbol{Duty}_{\mathrm{p3}}\ \mathrm{(NON)A}$$

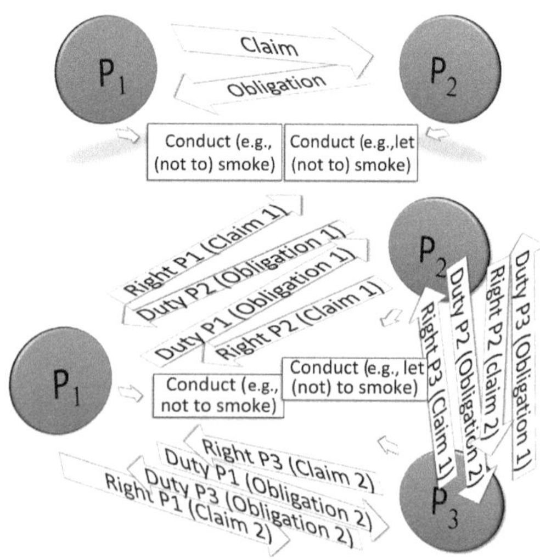

Legal norm $\left(P_{1,2\ldots claim(right)\rightarrow (no)act\leftarrow (duty)obl}P_{3,4\ldots}\right)$

DOI: 10.4324/9781003228318-5

Norms connect to constitute legal systems (that is, legal persons) through procedure, which can be defined as a sequence of acts (active or inactive conduct) performed in a specific time lapse $\left(P_{\rightarrow(\text{no})\text{act}(t1)\rightarrow} P_{\rightarrow(\text{no})\text{act}(t2)}\right)$, either vertically, based on hierarchy $\left(P_{\rightarrow(\text{no})\text{act}\rightarrow} P\text{—}P \rightarrow P\text{—}P\right)$, or horizontally, notably based on the imputation (causation) principle (primary obligation (1) (P—P) → breach → sanction (secondary obligation (P—P) (2)) : $(1)P - P_{\rightarrow\text{breach}\rightarrow} P - P(2)$).

$$\boldsymbol{Obl}_{p1}\,(\text{NON})\text{A} - \boldsymbol{Claim}_{p2}\,(\text{NON})\text{A} \rightarrow \boldsymbol{Obl}_{p1}\,(\text{NON})\text{A} - \boldsymbol{Claim}_{p2}\,(\text{NON})\text{A}$$
$$\boldsymbol{Obl}_{p1}\,(\text{NON})\text{A} - \boldsymbol{Claim}_{p2}\,(\text{NON})\text{A} \rightarrow \boldsymbol{Obl}_{p1}\,(\text{NON})\text{A} - \boldsymbol{Claim}_{p2}\,(\text{NON})\text{A}$$

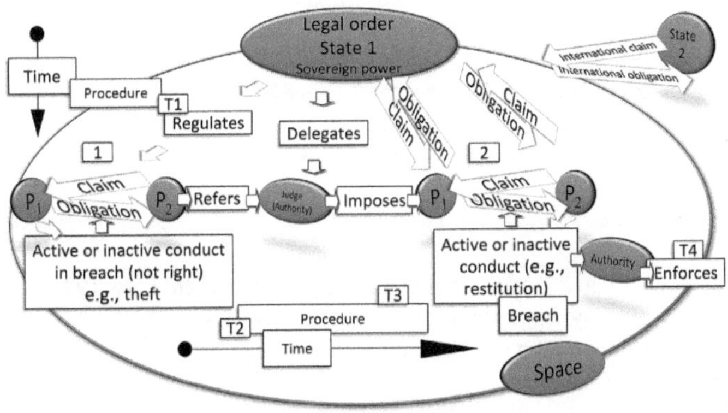

Legal system $\left(P_{\rightarrow\text{law-making}} \rightarrow P\text{—}P_{\rightarrow} P\text{—}P_{\rightarrow\text{breach}\rightarrow} P_{\rightarrow\text{settlement}\rightarrow} P\text{—}P_{\rightarrow\text{breach}\rightarrow} P_{\rightarrow\text{enforcement}}\right)$

Such a methodology, based on minimalistic (ABC) deontic concepts, permits elaborating a purely formal representation of the legal system and its subsystems, including the State, international law and EU law, as (procedural) deontic networks. These formal (procedural) neural processes can be combined and extended indefinitely.[1]

1 'All those moments will be lost in time, like tears in rain' (*Blade Runner*, Tears in Rain Monologue, 1982).

Documents

Antarctic Treaty, opened for signature 1 December 1959, 402 UN Treaty Series 71, entered into force 23 June 1961.

Articles of Agreement of the International Bank for Reconstruction and Development, opened for signature 22 July 1944, 2 UN Treaty Series 39, entered into force 27 December 1945.

Charter of the International Military Tribunal, Nuremberg, adopted 8 August 1945.

Charter of the International Military Tribunal for the Far East, Tokyo, adopted 19 January 1946.

Charter of the United Nations, opened for signature 26 June 1945, 1 UN Treaty Series 16, entered into force 24 October 1945.

Commonwealth of Australia, Uniform Evidence Act, 1995.

Convention on Contracts for the International Sale of Goods, opened for signature 11 April 1980, 1489 UN Treaty Series 3, entered into force 1 January 1988.

Convention on International Civil Aviation, opened for signature 7 December 1944, 15 UN Treaty Series 295, entered into force 4 April 1947.

Convention on the High Seas, opened for signature 29 April 1958, 450 UN Treaty Series 82, entered into force 30 September 1962.

Convention on the Law Applicable to Contractual Obligations, opened for signature 19 June 1980, 19 International Legal Materials 1492, entered into force 1 April 1991.

Convention on the Law of the Sea, opened for signature 10 December 1982, 1833 UN Treaty Series 396, entered into force 16 November 1994.

Convention on the Recognition and Enforcement of Foreign Arbitral Awards, opened for signature 10 June 1958, 330 UN Treaty Series 38, entered into force 7 June 1959.

Convention Relating to the Regulation of Aerial Navigation, opened for signature 13 October 1919, no longer in force.

COPUOS, Definition and Delimitation of Outer Space, UN Doc. A/AC.105/C.2/2022/CRP.24, 6 April 2022.

Declaration of the First Meeting of Equatorial Countries, 3 December 1976.

European Commission, Implementing Decision (EU) 2016/1189 of 19 July 2016 Authorising the Placing on the Market of UV-treated Milk as a Novel Food under Regulation (EC) No. 258/97 of the European Parliament and of the Council, 196 OJ L 50.

European Parliament and Council, Directive 2003/88/EC of 4 November 2003 Concerning Certain Aspects of the Organisation of Working Time, 299 OJ L 9.

European Parliament and Council, Regulation of 25 October 2011 on the Provision of Food Information to Consumers, Doc. 02011R1169-20140219.

European Parliament and EU Council, Law Applicable to Non-contractual Obligations, Regulation (EC) No. 864/2007.

European Parliament, Council and Commission, Joint Declaration on Practical Arrangements for the Co-decision Procedure (2007) OJ C145/5.

General Agreement on Trade and Tariffs, opened for signature 30 October 1947, 55 UN Treaty Series 194, entered into force 1 June 1948.

ILC, Report on the Work of Its Sixty-Third Session (2011) *ILC Yearbook* 1.

Marrakesh Agreement Establishing the World Trade Organization, opened for signature 15 April 1994, 1867 UN Treaty Series 154, entered into force 1 January 1995.

Montevideo Convention on the Rights and Duties of States, opened for signature 26 December 1933, 165 League of Nations Treaty Series 19, entered into force 26 December 1934.

Statute of the International Court of Justice, opened for signature 26 June 1945, 1 UN Treaty Series XVI, entered into force 24 October 1945.

Statute of the International Criminal Court, opened for signature 27 July 1998, 2187 UN Treaty Series 2, entered into force 1 July 2002.

Treaty Establishing a Constitution for Europe, 29 October 2004.

Treaty Establishing the European Atomic Energy Community, opened for signature 25 March 1957, 298 UN Treaty Series 259, entered into force 1 January 1958.

Treaty Establishing the European Coal and Steel Community, opened for signature 18 April 1951, 261 UN Treaty Series 140, entered into force 23 July 1952, expired 23 July 2002.

Treaty Establishing the European Economic Community, opened for signature 25 March 1997, 298 UN Treaty Series 3, entered into force 1 January 1958.

Treaty of Lisbon Amending the Treaty on European Union and the Treaty Establishing the European Community, opened for signature 13 December 2007, 2702 UN Treaty Series 3 No. 47938, entered into force 1 December 2009.

Treaty on European Union, opened for signature 7 February 1992, 31 International Legal Materials 247, entered into force 1 November 1993.

Treaty on Principles Governing the Activities of States in the Exploration and Use of Outer Space, Including the Moon and Other Celestial Bodies, opened for signature 27 January 1967, 610 UN Treaty Series 205, entered into force 10 October 1967.

UK, Withdrawal Agreement (from the EU), notified 29 March 2017, entered into force 31 January 2020.

UN Security Council, Establishment of the International Criminal Tribunal for Rwanda, Resolution 955/1994.

UN Security Council, Establishment of the International Criminal Tribunal for the Former Yugoslavia, Resolution 827/1993.

Cases

Barcelona Traction, Light and Power Company, Limited (New Application: 1962) (Belgium v. Spain) Second Phase (Judgment) [1970] ICJ Reports 3.

Frontier Dispute (Burkina Faso v. Republic of Mali) (Judgment) [1986] ICJ Reports 554.

Furundžija, IT- 95–17/1, Trial Chamber, Judgment of 10 December 1998.

Interpretation of the Agreement of 25 March 1951 between the WHO and Egypt (Advisory Opinion) [1950] ICJ Reports 73.

Island of Palmas (Netherlands v. U.S.), Award of 4 April 1928 (1928) II Reports of International Arbitral Awards 829.

Legality of the Use by a State of Nuclear Weapons in Armed Conflict (Advisory Opinion) [1996] ICJ Reports 66.

M/V 'Saiga' (Saint Vincent and the Grenadines v. Guinea) (No. 2), International Tribunal for the Law of the Sea (ITLOS), Judgment of 1 July 1999 (1999) ITLOS Reports 10.

Military and Paramilitary Activities in and against Nicaragua (Nicaragua v. United States of America) (Judgment) [1986] ICJ Reports 14.

Payment of Various Serbian Loans Issued in France (France v. Serbia) (Judgment) [1929] PCIJ Series A No. 20, 3.

Reparation for Injuries Suffered in the Service of the United Nations (Advisory Opinion) [1949] ICJ Reports 174.

S.S. Lotus (France v. Turkey) [1927] PCIJ Series A No. 10, 4.

Texaco Overseas Petroleum Company/California Asiatic Oil Company v. the Government of the Libyan Arab Republic (Compensation for Nationalized Property), Award (1978) 17(1) International Legal Materials 1.

Van Gend and Loos, ECJ, Case 26/61, Judgment of 5 February 1963 [1963] ECR 00003.

Vita Food Products Inc v. Unus Shipping Company Ltd. [1939] AC 277.

Bibliography

Abdi, H., Valentin, D. and Edelman, B., *Neural Networks*, Sage University Press, 1999.

Adam, B., *Time*, Polity Press, 2004.

Alchurrón, C.E. and Bulygin, E., *Normative Systems*, Springer, 1971.

Alexy, R., *Law's Ideal Dimension*, Oxford University Press, 2021.

Amerasinghe, F., *Principles of Institutional Law of International Organisations*, Cambridge University Press, 2nd ed., 2005.

Audoin, C. and Guinot, B., *The Measurement of Time: Time, Frequency and the Atomic Clock*, Cambridge University Press, 2001.

Austin, J., *Lectures on Jurisprudence: The Philosophy of Positive Law*, J. Murray, 4th ed., 1875.

Austin, J., *The Province of Jurisprudence Determined*, Murray, 1832, Weidenfeld & Nicolson, 1954.

Bailey, K.D., *Typologies and Taxonomies: An Introduction to Classification Techniques*, Sage, 1994.

Barbour, J., *The End of Time*, Oxford University Press, 2001.

Barbour, J., *The Janus Point: A New Theory of Time*, Basic Books, 2020.

Barbour, J., 'The Nature of Time' (2009) ArXiv:0903.3489v1 1.

Barnett, R.E., 'Contract Is Not a Promise; Contract Is Consent', in G. Klass, G. Letsas and P. Saprai (eds.), *Philosophical Foundations of Contract Law*, Oxford University Press, 2014, 41.

Bautzmann, A., *Atlals géopolitique mondial*, Rocher, 2024.

Belegu, M., 'Convention for International Sale of Goods in the Internal Law' (2021) 10(special) *Perspectives of Law and Public Administration* 113.

Bender, J. and Marrinan, M., *The Culture of Diagram*, Stanford University Press, 2010.

Bentham, J., *Works*, Bowring's ed., 1843.

Bentham, J., *A Fragment on Government*, 1776, Cambridge University Press, 1988.

Bergel, J.-L., *Théorie générale du droit*, LGDJ, 2003.

Bernal, C., Huerta, C., Mazzarese, T., Moreso, J.J., Navarro, P.E. and Paulson, S.L. (eds.), *Essays in Legal Philosophy*, Oxford University Press, 2015, 171.

Bertea, S., *The Normative Claim of Law*, Hart, 2009.

Birth, K., *Objects of Time: How Things Shape Temporality*, Palgrave, 2012.

Birth, K., 'Standards in the Shadows for Everyone to See: The Supranational Regulation of Time and the Concern over Temporal Pluralism', in S. Beynon-Jones and E. Grabham (eds.), *Law and Time*, Routledge, 2019, 106.

Black, M., 'The "Direction" of Time' (1959) 19(3) *Analysis* 54.

Bloom, F., 'The Law's Clock' (2015–2016) 104 *Georgetown Law Journal* 1.

Bobbio, N., *Teoria generale del diritto* (*General Theory of Law*), Giappichelli, 1993.

Bobbio, N., *Essais de théorie du droit*, ed. M. Guéret, C. Agostini and R. Guastini, Bruylant, 1998.

Bodin, J., *Les six livres de la République*, Jacques du Puys, 1576.

Bongiovanni, G., Postema, G., Rotolo, A., Sartor, G., Valentini, C. and Walton, D. (eds.), *Handbook of Legal Reasoning and Argumentation*, Springer, 2018.

Bostanu, A., 'Transnational Law: A New System of Law?' (2021) 11(special issue) *Juridical Tribune* 332.

Bourdieu, P., *Sur l'État*, Seuil, 2012.

Brad Wray, K., 'Social Epistemology', in M. Curd and S. Psillos (eds.), *The Routledge Companion to Philosophy of Science*, Routledge, 2014, 112.

Brix, B., *Law, Language and Legal Determinacy*, Clarendon Press, 1993.

Bruun, H.H. and Whimster, S. (eds.), *Max Weber: Collected Methodological Writings*, Routledge, 2012.

Bulygin, E. and Alchurrón, C.E., 'Permissory Norms and Normative Systems', in C. Bernal, C. Huerta, T. Mazzarese, J.J. Moreso, P.E. Navarro and S.L. Paulson (eds.), *Essays in Legal Philosophy*, Oxford University Press, 2015a, 324.

Bulygin, E. and Alchurrón, C.E., 'The Silence of the Law', in C. Bernal, C. Huerta, T. Mazzarese, J.J. Moreso, P.E. Navarro and S.L. Paulson (eds.), *Essays in Legal Philosophy*, Oxford University Press, 2015b, 293.

Bulygin, E. and Alchurrón, C.E., 'Time and Validity', in C. Bernal, C. Huerta, T. Mazzarese, J.J. Moreso, P.E. Navarro and S.L. Paulson (eds.), *Essays in Legal Philosophy*, Oxford University Press, 2015c, 171.

Caillois, R. and McKeon, N., 'Circular Time, Rectilinear Time' (1963) 11(42) *Diogenes* 1.

Calhoun, C. and Rhote, D., 'Integrating the Social Sciences: Theoretical Knowledge, Methodological Tools, and Practical Applications', in R. Frodeman, J.T. Klein and C. Mitcham (eds.), *The Oxford Handbook of Interdisciplinarity*, Oxford University Press, 2010, 103.

Callender, C. (ed.), *The Oxford Handbook of Philosophy of Time*, Oxford University Press, 2011.

Campo, A. and Gozzano, S., *Einstein vs. Bergson: An Enduring Quarrel on Time*, De Gruyter, 2022.

Carbonnier, T., *Sociologie juridique*, 1979, PUF, 1994.

Carnap, R., *The Unity of Science*, Thoemmes Press, 1995.

Chang, Y. (ed.), *Law and Economics of Possession*, Cambridge University Press, 2015, 40.

Chen, C., Härdle, W. and Unwin, A., *Handbook on Data Visualization*, Springer, 2008.

Christian, D., *Maps of Time: An Introduction to Big History*, University of California Press, 2004.

Christiano, T., 'The Legitimacy of International Institutions', in A. Marmor (ed.), *The Routledge Companion to Philosophy of Law*, Routledge, 2012, 380.

Collier, J. and Lowe, V., *The Settlement of Disputes in International Law: Institutions and Procedures*, Oxford University Press, 1999.

Cook, W.W., '"Substance" and "Procedure" in the Conflict of Laws' (1933) 42 *Yale Law Journal* 333.

Costa, P. and Zolo, D., *The Rule of Law: History, Theory and Criticism*, Springer, 2007.

Curd, M. and Psillos, S. (eds.), *The Routledge Companion to Philosophy of Science*, Routledge, 2014.

Dabin, J., *Théorie générale du droit*, Dalloz, 1969.

Danilenko, G.M., 'International Law-Making for Outer Space' (2016) 37 *Space Policy* 179.

D'Avila Garcez, A.S., Broda, K.B. and Gabbay, D.M. (eds.), *Neural-Symbolic Learning Systems: Foundations and Applications*, Springer, 2002.

De Brabandere, E., 'International Adjudication and Jurisdictional Conflict', in U. Linderfalk (ed.), *The International Legal System as a System of Knowledge*, Edward Elgar, 2021, 182.

Dedek, H., 'Subjective Right(s)', in J.M. Smits, J. Husa, C. Valcke and M. Narciso (eds.), *Encyclopaedia of Comparative Law*, Edward Elgar, 2024, 449.

Del Mar, M., 'Philosophical Analysis and Historical Inquiry: Theorizing Normativity, Law and Legal Thought', in M.D. Dubber and C. Thomas (eds.), *The Oxford Handbook of Legal History*, Oxford University Press, 2008, 3.

Descartes, R., *Discours de la Méthode*, Ian Maire, 1637.

Diani, M., 'Political and Policy Networks', in J. McLevey, J. Scott and P.J. Carrington (eds.), *The Sage Handbook of Social Network Analysis*, Sage, 2024, 130.

Dietze, G., 'The Limited Rationality of Law', in C.G. Friedrich (ed.), *Rational Decision*, Transaction Publisher, 1964, 63.

Dimock, W.C., 'Time against Territoriality: National Laws and Literary Translations', in A. Sarat, L. Douglas and M.M. Umphrey (eds.), *The Place of Law*, The University of Michigan Press, 2009, 21.

Donlan, S.P. and Urscheler, L.H. (eds.), *Concepts of Law: Comparative, Jurisprudential, and Social Science Perspectives*, Ashgate, 2014.

Drago, R., 'La notion d'obligation: droit public et droit privé' (2000) 44 *Archives de philosophie du droit* 43.

Dubber, M.D. and Thomas, C., *The Oxford Handbook of Legal History*, Oxford University Press, 2008.

Dupuy, J.-P., *On the Origin of Cognitive Science: The Mechanisation of the Mind*, tr. M.B. DeBevoise, MIT Press, 2009.

Dworkin, R., *Law's Empire*, Hart, 1998.

Eddington, A.S., *The Nature of the Physical World*, Cambridge Scholar Publishing, 1927.

Einstein, A., Lorentz, H.A., Weil, H. and Minkowski, H., *The Principle of Relativity: A Collection of Original Memoirs on the Special and General Theory of Relativity*, Methuen, 1923.

Elliot, E. and Kiel, L.D. (eds.), *Complex Systems in the Social and Behavioural Sciences: Theory, Methods and Application*, University of Michigan Press, 2021.

Erciyes, K., *Complex Networks: An Algorithmic Perspective*, CRC, 2015.

Erlich, E., *Grundlegung der Soziologie des Rechts*, Dunker, 1913.

Estrada, E., *The Structure of Complex Networks: Theory and Applications*, Oxford University Press, 2012.

Ferrajoli, L., 'The Past and Future of the Rule of Law', in P. Costa and D. Zolo (eds.), *The Rule of Law: History, Theory and Criticism*, Springer, 2007, 323.

Feyerabend, P., *Problems of Empiricism*, Cambridge University Press, 1981a.

Feyerabend, P., *Realism, Rationalism and Scientific Method*, Cambridge University Press, 1981b.

Feyerabend, P., *Against Method*, New Left Books, 1975, Verso, 2002.

Feyerabend, P., *The Tyranny of Science*, Polity Press, 2011.

Foucault, M., *Surveiller et punir*, Gallimard, 1975.

Foucault, M., *Power*, tr. R. Hubley, et al., New York Press, 1994.

Fox-Decent, E., *Sovereignty's Promise: The State as a Fiduciary*, Oxford University Press, 2011.

Frändberg, Å., *From Rechtsstaat to Universal Law-State: An Essay in Philosophical Jurisprudence*, Springer, 2014.

Freeman, J.A., *Simulating Neural Networks with Mathematica*, Addison-Wesley, 1994.

Freeman, M. and Smith, F., *Law and Language*, Oxford University Press, 2013.

Frege, W.G., 'Conceptual Notation' (1879), in A. Sullivan (ed.), *Logicism and the Philosophy of Language*, Broadview Press, 2003, 93.

Fried, M., 'Art and Objecthood' (1967) 6(2) *Artforum* 12.

Friedrich, C.G. (ed.), *Rational Decision*, Transaction Publisher, 1964.

Fukuyama, F., *The End of History and the Last Man*, Free Press, 1992.

Gentili, P.L., *Untangling Complex Systems*, CRC Press, 2019.

Giddens, A., *The Constitution of Society*, Polity Press, 1984.

Goetz, K.H. (ed.), *The Oxford Handbook of Time and Politics*, Oxford University Press, 2019.

Gregg, J. R. and Harris, F.T.C. (eds.), *Form and Strategy in Science*, D. Reided Publishing Company, 1964.

Grotius, H., *De jure belli ac pacis (On the Law of War and Peace)*, 1625, tr. A.C. Campbell, Createspace, 2017.

Habermas, J., *Zur Logik der Sozialwissenschaften (On the Logic of Social Sciences)*, Suhrkamp Verlag, 1982, tr. S.W. Nicholsen and J.A. Stark, Polity Press, 1988.

Hall, D.E., *Criminal Law and Procedure*, Cengage Learning, 7th ed., 2014.

Halpin, A., 'Language, Truth and Law', in M. Freeman and F. Smith (eds.), *Law and Language*, Oxford University Press, 2013, 62.

Hart, H., *The Concept of Law*, 1961, Clarendon Press, 3rd ed., 2012.
Hayek, F., *The Constitution of Liberty*, 1960, Routledge, reprinted 2008.
Healy, K., *Data Visualization*, Princeton University Press, 2019.
Hegel, G.W.F., *Philosophie des Rechts (Philosophy of Rights)*, 2021, tr. S.W. Dyde, Batoche Books, 2001.
Heidegger, M., *Sein und Zeit (Being and Time)*, Max Niemeyer Verlag, 1953, tr. J. Stambaugh, State University of New York Press, 1996.
Heiss, H. (ed.), *Kant: Political Writings*, Cambridge University Press, 1991.
Heraclitus, *Fragments*, Penguin Putnam, 2003.
Hetcher, S.A., *Norms in a Wired World*, Cambridge University Press, 2004.
Heyck, H., *Age of Systems*, John Hopkins University Press, 2015.
Hirsch, T., *Le temps des sociétés: d'Émile Durkheim à Marc Bloch*, EHESS, 2012.
Hobbes, T., *Leviathan*, 1651, ed. N. Malcolm, Clarendon Press, 2012, Vol. 2.
Hohfeld, W.N., 'Some Fundamental Legal Conceptions as Applied in Judicial Reasoning' (1913) *Yale Law Journal* 16.
Holland, T.E., *The Elements of Jurisprudence*, MacMillan, 1880.
Holtung, N. and Lippert-Rasmussen, K. (eds.), *Egalitarianism: New Essays on the Nature and Value of Equality*, Oxford University Press, 2007.
Houser, N. and Kloesel, C.J.W. (eds.), *The Essential Peirce*, Indiana University Press, 1992 and 1998.
Hume, D., *A Treatise of Human Nature*, 1739, Clarendon Press, 1896.
Humphreys, S., *Theatre of the Rule of Law: Transnational Legal Intervention in Theory and Practice*, Cambridge University Press, 2010.
Husserl, E., *Formale und transzendentale Logik. Versuch einer Kritik der logischen Vernunft (Formal and Transcendental Logic)*, 1929, tr. T.D. Carins, Springer, 1969.
Jackson, B.S., *Semiotics and Legal Theory*, Routledge and Keagan Paul, 1985.
Kalinowski, J., *Études de logique déontique I, 1953–1969*, Gallica, 1972.
Kant, I., 'Die Metaphysik der Sitten (The Metaphysics of Morals)', 1797, tr. H.B. Nisbeth, in H. Heiss (ed.), *Kant: Political Writings*, Cambridge University Press, 1991, 131.
Kant, I., 'Die Metaphysik der Sitten (Groundwork of the Metaphysics of Morals)', 1797, in *Practical Philosophy: Works of Immanuel Kant*, tr. M. Gregor, Cambridge University Press, 1997, 37.
Kawaguchi, K.H., *A Social Theory of International Law: International Relations as a Complex System*, Springer, 2003.
Kelsen, H., *General Theory of Law and State*, Russell & Russell, 1945.
Kelsen, H., *Principles of International Law*, Rinehart & Company, 1952.
Kelsen, H., *Reine Rechtslehre* (*Pure Theory of Law*), UC Press, 1934, tr. M. Knight, 1989.
Kelsen, H., *Allgemeine Theorie der Normen (General Theory of Norms)*, Main Verlag, 1979, Oxford University Press, 1991.
Kelsen, H., *Reine Rechtslehre (Introduction to the Problems of Legal Theory)*, F. Duticke, 1934, tr. Paulson, Clarendon Press, 1992.
Kevelson, R., *The Law as a System of Signs*, Plenum Publishing, 1988.
Kincaid, H., 'Social Sciences', in M. Curd and S. Psillos (eds.), *The Routledge Companion to Philosophy of Science*, Routledge, 2014, 672.

Kirk, A., *Data Visualisation: A Handbook for Data Driven Design*, Sage, 2016.

Klass, G., Letsas, G. and Saprai, P. (eds.), *Philosophical Foundations of Contract Law*, Oxford University Press, 2014.

Knoke, D. and Kulinski, J.H., *Network Analysis*, Sage, 1982.

Knoke, D. and Yang, S., *Social Network Analysis*, Sage, 2020.

Kocourek, A., *An Introduction to the Science of Law*, Cambridge University Press, 1930.

Kocourek, A., 'Substance and Procedure' (1941) 10 *Fordham Law Review* 157.

Kreuzer, M., 'Varieties of Time in Comparative Historical Analysis', in K.H. Goetz (ed.), *The Oxford Handbook of Time and Politics*, Oxford University Press, 2019, 197.

Kripke, S., 'Semantical Considerations on Modal Logic' (1963) 16 *Acta Philosophica Fennica* 83.

Kripke, S., *Philosophical Troubles*, Oxford University Press, 2011.

Kurki, V.A.J., *A Theory of Legal Personhood*, Oxford University Press, 2019.

Kurki, V.A.J., *Legal Personhood*, Cambridge University Press, 2023.

Kwa, C., *Styles of Knowing: A New History of Science from Ancient Times to the Present*, Pittsburgh Press, 2021.

Kwiecień, R., 'The Formal Sources of International Law, the Relationship between Treaties and Custom, and the International Law-Making Process' (2022) 40(1) *Australian Yearbook of International Law* 46.

La Torre, M., *Law as Institution*, Springer, 2010.

Landes, D.S., *Revolution in Time: Clocks and the Making of the Modern World*, Belknap Press of Harvard University Press, 2000.

Lee, C., 'The Game of Go: Bounded Rationality and Artificial Intelligence', in E. Elliot and L.D. Kiel (eds.), *Complex Systems in the Social and Behavioural Sciences: Theory, Methods and Application*, University of Michigan Press, 2021, 157.

Lenaerts, K., *EU Procedural Law*, Oxford University Press, 2nd ed., 2023.

Levinas, E., 'Liberté et commandement' (1953) 58(3) *Revue de Métaphysique et de Morale* 264.

Levine, J., 'GPS and the Legal Traceability of Time' (2001) *GPS World* 52.

Leyland, P. and Anthony, G., *Administrative Law*, Oxford University Press, 8th ed., 2016.

Libchaber, R., *L'ordre juridique et le discours du droit: Essai sur les limites de la connaissance du droit*, LGDJ, 2013.

Linderfalk, U. (ed.), *The International Legal System as a System of Knowledge*, Edward Elgar Publishing, 2021.

Llewellyn, K.N., *The Theory of Rules*, University of Chicago Press, 2011.

Lloyd, H.A., 'How to Do Things With Signs: Semiotics in Legal Theory, Practice, and Education' (2021) 55 *University of Richmond Law Review* 861.

Locke, J., *Two Treatises of Government*, 1690, C. Baldwin, 1824.

Lopez-Claros, A., Dahl, A.L. and Groff, M., *Global Governance and the Emergence of Global Institutions for the 21st Century*, Cambridge University Press, 2020.

Lucas, R., 'On the Mechanics of Economic Development' (1988) 22(1) *Journal of Monetary Economics* 3.

Luhmann, N., *Das Recht der Gesellschaft (Law as a Social System)*, Suhrkamp,1993, tr. K.A. Ziegert, Oxford University Press, 2004.

Luhmann, N., *Die Gesellschaft der Gesellschaft (Theory of Society)*, 1997, Suhrkamp, tr. R. Barrett, Stanford University Press, 2013, Vol. I.

Lukic, R., *Théorie de l'Etat et du droit*, Dalloz, 1974.

Machiavelli, N., *De Principatibus (The Prince)*, 1513, tr. T. Parks, Penguin, 2009.

Mäki, U., 'Economics', in M. Curd and S. Psillos (eds.), *The Routledge Companion to Philosophy of Science*, Routledge, 2014, 621.

Marcuse, R., *One-dimensional Man: Studies in the Ideology of Advanced Industrial Society*, Beacon Press, 1964.

Marmor, A., *The Routledge Companion to Philosophy of Law*, Routledge, 2012.

Marmor, A., *The Language of Law*, Oxford University Press, 2014.

Marx, K., 'Economic and Philosophical Manuscripts', 1844, in D. McLellan (ed.), *Marx: Selected Writings*, Oxford University Press, 1977, 75.

Mattila, H.E.S., 'Legal Vocabulary', in P.M. Tiersma and L.M. Solan (eds.), *The Oxford Handbook of Language and Law*, Oxford University Press, 2012, 27.

Maudlin, T., *Philosophy of Physics: Space and Time*, Princeton University Press, 2012.

Mavroidis, C., *The WTO Dispute Settlement System: How, Why and Where?* Edward Elgar, 2022.

McBride, N.J. and Bagshaw, R., *Tort Law*, Pearson, 6th ed., 2018.

McCarthy, D. and Seidelmann, P.K., *Time: From Earth Rotation to Atomic Physics*, Cambridge University Press, 2nd ed., 2018.

McGee, K. and Latour, B., *The Normativity of Networks*, Routledge, 2014.

McIntyre, L.J., *Law in the Sociological Enterprise*, Westview Press, 1994.

McLellan, D. (ed.), *Marx: Selected Writings*, Oxford University Press, 1977.

McLevey, J., Scott, J. and Carrington, P.J. (eds.), *The Sage Handbook of Social Network Analysis*, Sage, 2024.

Merriam, G., Merriam, C. and Webster, N., Dictionary, https://www.merriam-webster.com.

Merriam, P., 'A Theory of the Big Bang in McTaggart's Time' (2022) 32(suppl. 3) *Axiomathes* S685.

Messenger, G., 'The Development of International Law, Perception and the Problem of Time', in K.P. Van der Ploeg, L. Pasquet and L. Castellanos-Jankiewicz (eds.), *International Law and Time: Narratives and Techniques*, Springer, 2022, 335.

Mill, J.S., *On Liberty*, 1859, Yale University Press, 2003.

Moore, T., *Utopia*, 1513, tr. D. Baker-Smith, Penguin, 2012.

Morgenthau, H.J., *Politics Among Nations: The Struggle for Power and Peace*, Knopf, 1948.

Muir Watt, H. (ed.), *Private International Law and Public Law*, Edward Elgar, 2015.

Müller-Mall, S., *Legal Spaces: Towards a Topological Thinking of Law*, Springer, 2013.

Naffine, N., *Law's Meaning of Life: Philosophy, Religion, Darwin and the Legal Person*, Hart Publishing, 2009.

Namboodiri, K., *Matrix Algebra: An Introduction*, Sage, 1984.
Navarro, P.E. and Rodrigues, J.L., *Deontic Logic and Legal Systems*, Cambridge University Press, 2014.
Negro, A., *Graph-Powered Machine Learning*, Manning Publications, 2021.
Newman, M., *Networks: An Introduction*, Oxford University Press, 2010.
Newman, M., Barabási, A.-L. and Watts, D.J. (eds.), *The Structure and Dynamics of Networks*, Princeton University Press, 2006.
Nicolas, E., *Penser les flux normatifs: essai sur le droit fluide*, Mare & Martin, 2018.
Nietzsche, F., *Genealogy of Morals*, Broadview Press, 1887.
Nietzsche, F., *Menschliches, Allzumenschliches: Ein Buch für freie Geister (Human, All Too Human: A Book for Free Spirits)*, 1878, tr. R.J. Hollingdale, Cambridge University Press, 1986.
Nijman, J.E., *The Concept of International Legal Personality: An Inquiry into the History and Theory of International Law*, TMC Asser Press, 2004.
Novelli, C., Bongiovanni, G. and Sartor, G., 'A Conceptual Framework for Legal Personality and Its Application to AI' (2022) 13(2) *Jurisprudence* 194.
Nozick, R., *Anarchy, State and Utopia*, Basic Books, 1974.
Nozick, R., *Philosophical Explanations*, Clarendon Press, 1981.
Nozick, R., *Socratic Puzzles*, Harvard University Press, 1997.
Ockham, W. (of), *Summa Totius Logicae*, 1323.
Peirce, C.S., 'How to Make Our Ideas Clear', 1878, in N. Houser and C. Kloesel (eds.), *The Essential Peirce*, Indiana University Press, Vol. I, 1992a, 124.
Peirce, C.S., 'On the Algebra of Logic: A Contribution to the Philosophy of Notation' (1880), in N. Houser and C. Kloesel (eds.), *The Essential Peirce*, Indiana University Press, Vol. I, 1992b, 225.
Peirce, C.S., 'An Outline Classification of the Sciences', 1903, in N. Houser and C. Kloesel (eds.), *The Essential Peirce*, Indiana University Press, Vol. II, 1998a, 258.
Peirce, C.S., 'New Elements (*Καινὰ στοιχεία*)', 1904, in N. Houser and C. Kloesel (eds.), *The Essential Peirce*, Indiana University Press, Vol. II, 1998b, 300.
Peirce, C.S., 'Of Reasoning in General', 1895, in N. Houser and C. Kloesel (eds.), *The Essential Peirce*, Indiana University Press, Vol. II, 1998c, 11.
Peirce, C.S., 'What is a Sign?', 1894, in N. Houser and C. Kloesel (eds.), *The Essential Peirce*, Indiana University Press, Vol. II, 1998d, 4.
Perelman, C., *Études de logique juridique*, Bruylant, 1978, Vol. VII.
Perrin, J.-F., *Pour une théorie de la connaissance juridique*, Droz, 1979.
Peterson, C., *De la logique des obligations, des permissions et des interdictions: de Von Wright à aujourd'hui*, Presses de l'Université de Montréal, 2016.
Pietrzykowsky, T., 'Law, Persons and the Discontents of Juridical Humanism', in T. Pietrzykowsky and B. Stancioli (eds.), *New Approaches to the Personhood in Law: Essays in Legal Philosophy*, Peter Lang GmbH, Internationaler Verlag der Wissenschaften, 2016, 13.

Pietrzykowsky, T. and Stancioli, B. (eds.), *New Approaches to the Personhood in Law: Essays in Legal Philosophy*, Peter Lang GmbH, Internationaler Verlag der Wissenschaften, 2016a.

Pietrzykowsky, T. and Stancioli, B., 'Modern Challenges to the Concept of a Person in Law', in T. Pietrzykowsky and B. Stancioli (eds.), *New Approaches to the Personhood in Law: Essays in Legal Philosophy*, Peter Lang GmbH, Internationaler Verlag der Wissenschaften, 2016b, 7.

Pirie, F., *The Rule of Laws: A 4,000-Year Quest to Order the World*, Basic Books, 2021.

Poincaré, H., *The Value of Science*, Science Press, 1907.

Pooley, O., 'Space and Time', in M. Curd and S. Psillos (eds.), *The Routledge Companion to Philosophy of Science*, Routledge, 2014, 507.

Popper, K., *Conjectures and Refutations: The Growth of Scientific Knowledge*, 1993, Routledge, reprint 2004.

Prell, C., *Social Network Analysis*, Sage, 2012.

Prell, C., Hollway, J., Matous, P. and Todo, Y., 'International Trade Networks', in J. McLevey, J. Scott and P.J. Carrington (eds.), *The Sage Handbook of Social Network Analysis*, Sage, 2024, 350.

Prell, C. and Schaefer, D.R., 'An Introduction to Social Network Analysis', in J. McLevey, J. Scott and P.J. Carrington (eds.), *The Sage Handbook of Social Network Analysis*, Sage, 2024a, 19.

Prell, C. and Schaefer, D.R., *Introducing Social Network Analysis*, Sage, 2024b.

Price, H., 'The Flow of Time', in C. Callender (ed.), *The Oxford Handbook of Philosophy of Time*, Oxford University Press, 2011, 276.

Quirico, O., *The International Legal System*, Thomson Reuters, 2020.

Radbruch, G., *Rechts-Philosophie*, K.F. Koehler Verlag, 1975.

Radbruch, G., *Einführung in die Rechtswissenschaft*, K.F. Koehler Verlag, 1980.

Ranchordás, S. and Roznai, Y. (eds.), *Time, Law and Change: An Interdisciplinary Study*, Bloomsbury, 2020.

Rawls, J., *A Theory of Justice*, Belknap Press at Harward University Press, revised ed., 1999.

Raz, J., *The Concept of a Legal System*, Clarendon Press, 1980.

Raz, J., *Practical Reason and Norms*, Princeton University Press, 1970, Oxford University Press, 2002.

Raz, J., *The Authority of Law*, Oxford University Press, 2nd ed., 2009.

Read, W., *Legal Thinking: Its Limits and Tensions*, University of Pennsylvania Press, 1986.

Richards, E.G., *Mapping Time: The Calendar and Its History*, Oxford University Press, 1998.

Ricoeur, P., 'Herméneutique et sciences sociales', in P. Amselek (ed.), *Théorie du droit et science*, PUF, 1994, 15.

Roberts, L., 'A Lost Connection: Geostationary Satellite Networks and the International Telecommunication Union' (2000) 15(3) *Berkeley Technology Law Journal* 1095.

Romano, S., *L'ordinamento giuridico (The Legal Order)*, 1917, tr. M. Croce, Routledge, 2017.

Rooney, D., *About Time: A History of Civilization in Twelve Clocks*, W.W. Norton and Company, 2021.

Rose, C.M., 'The Law Is Nine-Tenths of Possession: An Adage Turned on Its Head', in Y. Chang (ed.), *Law and Economics of Possession*, Cambridge University Press, 2015, 40.

Ross, A., *Om ret og retfærdighed (On Law and Justice)*, 1953, University of California Press, 1958.

Rotolo, A. and Sartor, G., 'Deductive and Deontic Reasoning', in G. Bongiovanni, G. Postema, A. Rotolo, G. Sartor, C. Valentini and D. Walton (eds.), *Handbook of Legal Reasoning and Argumentation*, Springer, 2018, 243.

Roughan, N., *Authorities: Conflicts, Cooperation, and Transnational Legal Theory*, Oxford University Press, 2013.

Rousseau, J.J., *Discours sur l'origine et les fondements de l'inégalité parmi les hommes*, M.M. Rey, 1755.

Rousseau, J.J., *Du contrat social, ou principes du droit politique*, M.M. Rey, 1762.

Russell, B., *Power: A New Social Analysis*, Allen and Unwin Ltd., 1938.

Sainsbury, M., *Logical Forms: An Introduction to Philosophical Logic*, Blackwell, 2nd ed., 2001.

Salmond, J., *Jurisprudence*, Sweet & Maxwell, 6th ed., 1924.

Sankey, H., 'Scientific Method', in M. Curd and S. Psillos (eds.), *The Routledge Companion to Philosophy of Science*, Routledge, 2014, 280.

Sarat, A., Douglas, L. and Umphrey, M.M. (eds.), *The Place of Law*, The University of Michigan Press, 2009.

Sartor, G., 'Fundamental Legal Concepts: A Formal and Teleological Characterisation' (2006) 14 *AI & Law* (2006) 101.

Sartor, G., *Legal Reasoning: A Cognitive Approach to the Law*, Springer, 2007.

Sartor, G., Casanovas, P., Biasiotti, M.A. and Fernández-Barrera, M. (eds.), *Approaches to Legal Ontologies: Theories, Domains, Methodologies*, Springer, 2011.

Savigny, F.K., *Vom Beruf unserer Zeit für Gesetzgebung und Rechtswissenschaft*, Ben Mohr und Bimmer, 1814.

Scelle, G., *Précis de droit des gens: principes et systématique*, Sirey, 1932.

Schiff Berman, P., *Global Legal Pluralism*, Cambridge University Press, 2012.

Schmitt, C., *Die Diktatur: Von den Anfängen des modernen Souveränitätsgedankens bis zum proletarischen Klassenkampf (The Dictatorship: From the Origin of the Modern Concept of Sovereignty to Proletarian Class Struggle)*, 1921, tr. M. Hoelzel and G. Ward, Polity Press, 2014.

Scott, J., *Social Network Analysis*, Sage, 2017.

Sen, A., *The Idea of Justice*, Belknap Press of Harvard University Press, 2009.

Sériaux, A., *Le droit – Une introduction*, Ellipses, 1997.

Shelton, D., *Jus Cogens*, Oxford University Press, 2024.

Sinclair, M. (ed.), *Handbook of Research Methods on Intuition*, Edward Elgar, 2014.

Smits, J.M., Husa, J., Valcke, C. and Narciso, M., *Encyclopaedia of Comparative Law*, Edward Elgar, 2024.

Snijders, T.A.B. and Bosker, R.J., *Multilevel Analysis: An Introduction to Basic and Advanced Multilevel Modeling*, Sage, 2003.

Sonawane, S., Mahalle, P.N. and Ghotka, A.S. (eds.), *Information Retrieval and Natural Language Processing: A Graph Theory Approach*, Springer, 2022.

Sowa, J.F., *Knowledge Representation: Logical, Philosophical and Computational Representation*, Brooks/Cole, 2000.

Spinoza, B., *Tractatus Politicus (Political Treatise)*, 1676, Hackett, 2000.

Sullivan, A. (ed.), *Logicism and the Philosophy of Language*, Broadview Press, 2003.

Tanaka, Y., 'The Legal Consequences of Obligations *Erga Omnes* in International Law' (2021) 68(1) *Netherlands International Law Review* 1.

Thomas, E.W., *The Judicial Process: Realism, Pragmatism, Reasoning and Principles*, Cambridge University Press, 2005.

Tiersma, P.M. and Solan, L.M. (eds.), *The Oxford Handbook of Language and Law*, Oxford University Press.

Tuori, K., *Critical Legal Positivism*, Ashgate, 2002.

Van der Ploeg, K.P., 'International Law through Time: On Change and Facticity in International Law', in K.P. Van der Ploeg, L. Pasquet and L. Castellanos-Jankiewicz (eds.), *International Law and Time: Narratives and Techniques*, Springer, 2022, 313.

Van der Ploeg, K.P., Pasquet, L. and Castellanos-Jankiewicz, L., *International Law and Time: Narratives and Techniques*, Springer, 2022.

Van Hoecke, M., 'Do "Legal Systems" Exist? The Concept of Law and Comparative Law', in S.P. Donlan and L.H. Urscheler (eds.), *Concepts of Law: Comparative, Jurisprudential, and Social Science Perspectives*, Ashgate, 2014.

Van Orman Quine, W., 'On Simple Theories of a Complex World', in J.R. Gregg and F.T.C. Harris (eds.), *Form and Strategy in Science*, D. Reided Publishing Company, 1964, 47.

Van Riel, A.C.R. and Horvath, C., 'Conceptualizing Intuition as a Mental Faculty: Towards a "Critique of Intuitive Reason" and a Process Model of Intuition', in M. Sinclair (ed.), *Handbook of Research Methods on Intuition*, Edward Elgar, 2014, 42.

Varella, M.D., *Internationalization of Law: Globalization, International Law and Complexity*, Springer, 2014.

Virally, M., *La pensée juridique*, LGDJ, 1960.

Von Bertalanffy, L., *General System Theory: Foundations, Development, Applications*, G. Braziller, 2003.

Von Leibniz, G.W., 'On Natural Law', in P. Riley (ed.), *Leibniz: Political Writings*, Cambridge University Press, 2nd ed., 1988.

Von Leibniz, G.W., *Nova methodus discendae docendoquae jurisprudentiae*, 1667, Giuffré, 2012.

Von Pufendorf, S., *De Officio Hominis et Civis Juxta Legem Naturalem Libri Duo* (*On the Duty of Man and Citizen According to Natural Law)*, 1673, tr. M. Silverthorne, Cambridge University Press, 1991.

Von Wright, G.H., 'Deontic Logic' (1951) 60 *Mind* 1.

Walton, D., Reed, C. and Macagno, F., *Argumentation Schemes*, Cambridge University Press, 2008.

Wasserman, S. and Faust, K., *Social Network Analysis: Methods and Applications*, Cambridge University Press, 1999.

Weber, M., 'Die "Objektivität" sozialwissenschaftlicher und sozialpolitischer Erkenntnis (The Objectivity of Knowledge in Social Science and Social Policy' (1904), in H.H. Bruun and S. Whimster (eds.), *Max Weber: Collected Methodological Writings*, Routledge, 2012, 100.

Westerståhl, D., *Foundations of Logic: Completeness, Incompleteness, Computability*, CSLI Publications, 2023.

Whithead, A.N. and Russell, B., *Principia Mathematica*, Cambridge University Press, 1910–1913.

Wilschut, A., *Images of Time: The Role of a Historical Consciousness of Time in Learning History*, IAP, 2012.

Wise, S.M., 'Legal Personhood and the Nonhuman Rights Project' (2010) 17 *Animal Law Review* 1.

Wittgenstein, L., *Tractatus Logico-Philosophicus*, Cambridge University Press, 1922.

Zhang, Y. and Teng, Z., *Natural Language Processing: A Machine Learning Perspective*, Cambridge University Press, 2021.

Index